Research for Writers

The author

Ann Hoffmann has spent the greater part of her professional life working with or for writers. After a first job in publishing, she travelled widely in Europe and, on returning to England, spent four years as secretary/researcher to the well-known writer, the late Robert Henriques. In 1966 she established a research service for authors. She now lives in Bloomsbury, London, where she combines researching for others with writing her own books; these include *The Dutch: How They Live and Work*, *Bocking Deanery*, *Lives of the Tudor Age*, and *Majorca*.

In this expanded and revised edition of RESEARCH, Miss Hoffmann writes knowledgeably from personal experience on a variety of sources of information, on research methods, on some of the pitfalls to be avoided by the 'novice' researcher, and on the particular problems facing writers of fiction and non-fiction.

Research for Writers

Ann Hoffmann

A & C Black · London

First published under the title *Research for Writers* 1986
by A & C Black (Publishers) Ltd
35 Bedford Row, London WC1R 4JH
Reprinted with corrections 1987

Previously published under the title *Research: a hand-
book for writers and journalists*
First edition 1975 Midas Books
Second edition 1979 A & C Black (Publishers) Ltd.

British Library Cataloguing in Publication Data

Hoffmann, Ann
    Research for writers. —
    Expanded and rev.ed.
    1. Literature —— Research
    I. Title   II. Hoffmann, Ann.
    Research
    808.023   PN73

    ISBN 0-7136-2811-1

ISBN 0-7136-2811-1

Printed in Great Britain by
Whitstable Litho Ltd, Whitstable, Kent

Contents

Abbreviations used in this Book

AGRA   Association of Genealogists and Record Agents
BAC   Business Archives Council
BALH   British Association for Local History
BL   British Library
BLAISE   British Library Automated Information Service
BM   British Museum*
BN   *Bibliothèque Nationale*
BNB   *British National Bibliography*
DNB   *Dictionary of National Biography*
FFHS   Federation of Family History Societies
HMSO   Her Majesty's Stationery Office
ICA   International Council on Archives
IGI   International Genealogical Index
KIST   *Keyword Index to Serial Titles*
n.d.   no date
N.S.   New Style (dates)
O.S.   Old Style (dates)
P.C.C.   Prerogative Court of Canterbury (Wills)
P.C.Y.   Prerogative Court of York (Wills)
PRO   Public Record Office
SRL   Science Reference Library

Note: For the sake of brevity and to avoid the clumsy repetition of 'he' and 'she' throughout the book, writers/researchers are referred to by the one pronoun, 'he'. No offence is intended to the female person.

*On 1 July 1973 the former library departments of the British Museum were incorporated in the British Library Reference Division. Scholars and *habitués* of the Reading Room and Department of Manuscripts still use the old affectionate term, 'the BM'.

Author's note

When I embarked on this project in 1975 it was with the idea of setting down, for freelance writers faced with the daunting task of researching for publication for the first time, some practical notes on methods and sources that would start them off along the right lines and at the same time help them to avoid some of the pitfalls. Although the book has grown in the process, and this third edition has further enabled me to up-date and expand the text, it was never intended to be – nor, considering the vast sources available to the modern writer, could it ever be – more than a guide. No one researcher can do more than scratch the surface, let alone compile a comprehensive research manual.

Researching, like writing, is an individual, creative and selective process. It cannot be 'taught'. In his quest for original material – and who does not dream of stumbling upon a cache of hitherto unknown, unpublished papers or the answer to a problem that has baffled scholars for several generations? – the writer never ceases to learn. All the time he is probing, absorbing, adding to his store of knowledge of sources of information largely by trial and error. Either he has a 'nose' for it or he has not. If not, unless he has time on his hands, he would be well advised to use the services of a professional. An elementary grasp of sources can of course be gleaned from a textbook and a few days' intensive study in a good reference library; this has immense value as a springboard. After that he is on his own. Invariably he will find himself, at different stages of his research, thrust into the unaccustomed rôles of student, librarian, interviewer, detective and private investigator, and much else besides.

Throughout the compilation of this handbook, therefore, I have had in mind the many time-consuming problems likely to be encountered by a novice writer-researcher, whether he is concerned with fiction or non-fiction. I have dared to suggest, from my own experience, ways in which these problems may be tackled. I have, as it were, laid out on my work bench for fellow craftsmen to pick up, handle and use as they see fit all those tried and trusted reference tools that have served me well in the last twenty years, together with some newer, less tested, aids. They may not be the particular assortment that a colleague would select, being in the main drawn from my own research activities which have concentrated more on the factual, historical and biographical rather than on scientific or technical fields. But to me they have proved loyal and steadfast helpmates, and I am confident that they will in turn help others to solve some of those alarming and often seemingly insoluble conundrums that have the nasty habit of cropping up at the worst possible moment in every writer's working day. Hopefully, too, in the long term, there may result books and features and theses that are not only better researched, but researched with less stress and strain and burning of the midnight oil on the part of their authors.

I should like to take this opportunity to express my gratitude to the many librarians, archivists, curators, press and public relations officers and others who have so efficiently and courteously dealt with my enquiries on a multitude of subjects over the years. I am also indebted to several fellow writers and research colleagues who made constructive comments on the first two editions, some of whose suggestions are now incorporated.

Gradually, over the past decade, most of us have been getting accustomed to the new 'information technology'. We have all seen CEEFAX and ORACLE and PRESTEL, even if we do not yet have them ourselves on our television screens at home. No one who has embarked recently on research at a library or archives centre can have failed to make use of the up-to-date microfiche author/title or subject catalogues or one of several excellent reprographic facilities currently available. The regular researchers among us now know that if we require lengthy material to be photocopied or sent from overseas, microfilm will work out cheaper than xerox copies. Readers at the Public Record Office tap out their document requests with confidence on the computer terminals, while at the British Library an increasing number obtain the bibliographical references they need through the computer search service.

In the 1979 edition of this book I forecast that the microfilm reader would soon become as normal a piece of equipment in the writer's study as the typewriter then was. I was wrong. Writing now in 1985, it is clear that writers and journalists and researchers in large droves are investing, not so much in the humble microfilm reader, but in personal computers and word processors. Some individual researchers are even competing with libraries by going 'on-line' in order to have access to the already vast, and rapidly growing, data-bases in this country and overseas.

We writers and researchers of today should count ourselves fortunate to be living in the midst of what the librarians and information scientists call 'the information explosion', in which a computer-generated bonanza of information has become accessible at speed, and at relatively low cost, via 'on-line' retrieval systems worldwide. For all of us this is a bonanza indeed. Never before has so much research material been so instantly accessible.

I also stuck my neck out by predicting that the time was not far off when the writer would do his research without ever setting foot in library or record office, simply by summoning his source material onto a screen at home. That day has not yet come, but we *are* moving in its direction. Already the fortunate computer-owner who is 'on-line'* is able to call up onto his personal monitor bibliographical material on any given subject, from international data-bases housing literally millions of references. A logical next step will be for all printed texts to be fed automatically into the computer at the time of publication. It is unlikely, however, that any attempt will be made to store all texts previously published (a task that would involve going back to the time of Caxton). Thus for the historian and the biographer, for the writer of historical novels – or indeed for any author or journalist who writes about the past – research in the library and archives centre will, for some time yet, still be very much a part of his work routine. Thus, too, the techniques and sources outlined here will remain valid.

As in the two earlier editions, books mentioned in the text are listed alphabetically by title at the end of the relevant chapter rather than in one long bibliography at the end. Regrettably, it is not possible always to indicate those books which are out of print, as the situation changes constantly and reprints or new editions may become available during the lifetime of this handbook. Most of the out-of-print titles mentioned will be found in the larger public libraries or may be borrowed through the public library lending service; but researchers needing to use such books over a long period are recommended to 'shop around' for them in second-hand and antiquarian bookshops (and even jumble sales), or to ask a book-finding service to try to locate them (see page 37).

Inevitably, with so much new material to hand, some titles have had to be dropped in this edition. The rule of thumb which I have applied here has been to prune and discard what I personally consider to be 'dead wood' (titles that have been superseded by more up-to-date, improved works), but to retain those earlier books that

---

*For an explanation of 'on-line' and other related terms, see pages 13–14.

are still among the best on their subject. For example, I doubt very much that a researcher today would want to consult a book about London libraries published as long ago as 1964, whereas a novelist setting his story in England in the early 19th century definitely still needs to know of John Burnett's admirable Pelican *History of the Cost of Living*, so that he can ask for it at the library.

My mail-bag since the appearance of the first edition makes it clear that the handbook has been of use not only to the amateur and student for whom it was intended, and even on occasion to those who make a hobby of entering competitions, but also to the more experienced 'diggers' who – so they tell me – sometimes suffer from extraordinary lapses of memory or mental blocks which may result in their wasting precious time searching for information that in fact is close at hand in their own reference collection or in a local library. To all these people I dedicate this revised edition. In return, the greatest compliment they can pay me will be to *use the book as a working tool, to annotate it profusely, and to up-date it as their research requires*. For this purpose I have asked my publishers to include a few blank pages at the end for personal notes. If, by the time these pages are filled, the book is starting to come apart at the spine through constant usage, hopefully there may be a fourth edition in the pipeline. As before, comments and suggestions for future editions will be most gratefully received.

1

The Writer as Researcher

Every writer, unless he is creating a work of pure fantasy, has to do research. The nature and depth of that research will vary enormously, according to the subject of the work, the field of writing (factual article, novel, biography, history, thesis, children's story, etc.) and whether it is intended for the academic, popular or juvenile market. Whereas the scholar may have comparatively unlimited time (and probably also a research grant) which allows him to follow up pretty well every relevant line of enquiry in detail, the journalist's 'copy' must be on the sub-editor's desk at a given hour, and he is always pressed for time. Both texts must be correct, up-to-date and original – in other words, properly researched and well written.

In the end-product the academic work, with its notes and references, bibliography and index, may look to be the more meticulously researched, but this can be a deception: the 1,000-word newspaper or magazine article, in order to present its data in a convincing, accurate and readable way and to show that its author is fully conversant with the latest events and/or published studies on the subject, may well involve as much, and sometimes more, research in proportion to its length. Whatever the field of authorship, the writer has to know a great deal more than he actually puts into words if what he writes is to ring true – and this applies as strictly to fiction writers as to journalists and historians and biographers. Ernest Hemingway, in an interview published in *Paris Review* (Spring 1958), put this very well. 'I always try to write on the principle of the iceberg,' he said. 'There is seven-eighths of it under water for every part that shows. Anything you know you can eliminate and it only strengthens your iceberg. It is the part that doesn't show. If the writer omits something because he does not know it, then there is a hole in the story.'*

*The same author, in *Death in the Afternoon*, expounds on this theme at greater length in a memorable passage worthy of framing and hanging above every writer's desk. It will be found at the end of Chapter 16; in the paperback edition (Penguin Books, 1973) at pages 181-3.

In ideal circumstances an author would write only of what he knows. No one, however, can have first-hand knowledge of every trade or profession in which he wishes to place his characters; few can afford to visit all those far-off lands that they are tempted to use as 'local colour' in their work. In most short stories or novels or plays, therefore, there are bound to be some people, some situations, and some settings that are beyond the personal experience of the writer, and for which he must rely to some extent at least on second-hand material – that is to say, on what others before him have observed and recorded, on printed statistics and factual data, and often on the recollections of third parties. The writer of history or historical fiction has no choice but to rely on documentary sources, either in print or in manuscript. In all these instances the research done must be thorough and, as far as possible, undertaken *in the round* (i.e. from more than one angle, avoiding reliance on any one source), or the result will be cardboard people, cardboard backgrounds and a loss of credibility in what may otherwise be an excellent piece of writing.

The prime importance of researching thoroughly before going into print cannot be over-stressed. Once his reader's confidence has been lost, the author will have an uphill battle to regain it. All too often a disillusioned reader or bright schoolchild will write and tell him where he has gone wrong, or – which is worse – may write and tell his editor or publisher, which in turn destroys their confidence and is likely to influence their attitude to the author's future work.

It is dangerous to rely on only one source for a given piece of information, however authoritative that source may seem to be. Mistakes occur all too frequently in even the most erudite book. They may not be the original author's fault at all, but the result of slipshod proof-reading in the editor's office or a printer's error that occurred at a later stage, such as when the type-setter re-sets a line to incorporate the author's or publisher's corrections. The sad thing is that once they are in print, mistakes are bound to be copied in good faith by someone else, and that person's work in turn may well be used as source material by another, and so on, so that even if a correction is made in subsequent editions of the original work, the misprint in that first edition may be perpetrated *ad infinitum*. By 'misprints' in this context is meant the mis-spelling of a proper name, a mis-quotation or a wrong figure – the sort of error that would not necessarily be spotted by a reader. The other kind of mistake, known as a 'literal' in publishing and printing, which may be a character set up in the wrong fount, or upside down, or two characters trans-posed, and the more obvious spelling mistake are more likely to be spotted at proof-reading stage.

Such are the hazards of authorship that the writer of non-fiction would do well to keep constantly in his mind's eye as he works the image of future trusting generations of students and researchers relying on his text as an authoritative source.

For most modern writers time is a precious commodity. Gone for ever are those halcyon days when Samuel Johnson could speak of a man turning over half a library to make one book; since his day millions more books have been written and published, and our libraries, archive collections and record repositories now house a bewildering and ever-increasing conglomeration of printed, manu-script, microfilmed and recorded material. More than ever before has it become essential for the writer-researcher to organise his working hours to the best advantage. He must know where and how to get at the information he requires in the quickest, as well as the most efficient and economical, way. As the great Dr Johnson also said: 'Knowledge is of two kinds. We know a subject ourselves, or we know where we can find information about it.' While the specialist must know his pet subject inside out, there is no question but that for the general writer the knowledge of *where to go* to find what he needs is of the greater value. Quite apart from the fact that no one would want to become a walking encyclopedia, even if it were humanly possible to carry a mass of information on a variety of subjects in one's head all the time, most professional writers would agree that a sound knowledge of available sources (or, failing that, a reliable researcher on whose services they can call) allows them more time to concentrate on the creative activity. Nothing can be more distracting or more paralysing to the flow of ideas and their shaping into words than a nagging worry, 'Where on earth am I going to be able to find out about *that*?'

Seeking information implies curiosity, a characteristic inborn not only in the feline species but in the whole human race. We have all been researchers since we were in the cradle. Long before he can speak or read or write, a baby is obsessed by the desire to find out about the things around him. Attracted by the colour of an unknown object, he reaches out to touch it and, having seized it and found it pleasing to hold, usually puts it into his mouth. What does it feel like? Does it taste good? What is it made of? *What* is it? He has taken the first step along a path of discovery and enchantment that will last a lifetime. From that first childish desire to learn about objects, he progresses to curiosity about himself and his body, and then to other people and animals; from the happenings he observes in his immediate circle to those of history; through history to religion, and then to science and speculation about the future. He will never know it all, but if as he grows older he keeps alive his youthful sense of curiosity he will – especially if he becomes a writer – have endless resources on which to draw, and he will never be bored.

It is a well-known saying that a writer may be angry, disgusted, amused, uplifted or almost anything in between, and his work will be the better for it, but if he is bored it will be reflected in his writing. Robert Louis Stevenson held that life would be only a very dull and ill-directed theatre unless we had some interests in the piece. 'It is in virtue of his own desires and curiosities that any man continues to exist with even patience,' he wrote, 'that he is charmed by the look of things and people, and that he wakens every morning with a renewed appetite for work and pleasure. Desire and curiosity are the two eyes through which he sees the world in the most enchanted colours: it is they that make women beautiful or fossils interesting…'*

Because a writer's raw material is derived principally from a study of other human beings, their complex relationships, their strengths and weaknesses and idiosyncrasies, as well as their history, he can probably get away with being more openly curious than any other group of people – provided always that he does not offend by his looking or probing. The arts of observation without seeming to observe and of probing without seeming to probe are skills that can – and should – be acquired.

While most writers are also researchers, not all researchers are talented as writers. The prime function of the researcher is to seek information; that of the writer is more complicated, for his duty is both to impart knowledge and to give pleasure – in other words, to entertain as well as to instruct his reader. And just as a factual book can give pleasure to the reader by the manner in which it is written, so the most absorbing and entertaining of stories can impart knowledge. The one thing a writer must never do, under any circumstances, however, is to distort the truth for the sake of a good story.

Everything that comes within the writer's own experience is grist to the mill and should be stored away, ideally in note form or on tape, for future use. Ideas, an unusual turn of phrase, a gesture, a conversation overheard, brief descriptions of people or places, on-the-spot reports of events, even pain suffered (you think at the time you will always remember how it felt, but you rarely do): these will be of immense value, provided that they are kept in such a way that they can be turned up quickly when required. (Some practical suggestions for filing and storage are discussed on pages 17-20). Naturally it is not possible to predict years in advance what you are going to need, so that how much or how little is noted and filed must

---

*from the essay 'El Dorado' in *Virginibus Puerisque*.

be a decision for the individual writer, but it is a fact of life that once you throw something away, you need it. The Preface to Somerset Maugham's *A Writer's Notebook*, first published in 1949, makes interesting reading on this score, for the author admits that there were many years in which he made no notes at all, that he kept no record of his meetings with famous people. 'I never made a note of anything that I did not think would be useful to me at one time or another in my work,' he states, 'and though, especially in the early notebooks, I jotted down all kinds of thoughts and emotions of a personal nature, it was only with the intention of ascribing them sooner or later to the creatures of my invention. I meant my notebooks to be a storehouse of materials for future use and nothing else.' So spoke the short story writer and novelist. It would be unthinkable for a diarist or biographer to fail to record his meetings with famous people.

In the course of his researching life a writer will be faced with a variety of tasks. These may range from the simple checking of facts (dates, quotations, spellings, statistics) to the tracing of a contemporary account of some historical event, or the more complicated unravelling of someone's ancestry, or an authentic setting for a novel or play. The best-selling author Frederick Forsyth reckons to divide his research into four categories: *geographical* (which necessitates visits to places); *historical* (checkable in source material); *procedural* (which involves contacting and talking to 'inside' people); and *technical* (checkable facts). It will be obvious that there are wide differences, both of skill and approach, between the four, and that some of the categories overlap or merge.

In *factual research* (statistical, historical and technical), the enquirer knows precisely what he is looking for and what he expects to find, so that, provided he knows where to go for the information, he should encounter no great difficulty. Knowing where to go is the key here.

In pure *historical research* the scope is much wider, both as regards the material available and the use that is made of it. As no two writers, given the same plot and the same set of characters, will come up with an identical story, so no two researchers, confronted with the same documentary sources, will use those sources in an identical way. The basic facts – the skeleton – will be similar, of course, but whereas one researcher will explore a certain avenue in more detail than another and quote extensively from a document that in the eyes of his colleague merits no more than a passing reference, the second may be less selective on one aspect of the search but obsessive about detail on another, depending upon the angle from which their respective works are to be written and on the market for which they are intended.

Background research (which includes the geographical and proce-.

dural), usually required for a work of fiction, modern or historical, generally demands less discipline but, as a result, may lead the enquirer down some unforeseen channels and possibly end by radically changing the shape or character of his story.

Thus both historical and background research fall into the category of *creative*, as opposed to *factual*, research. In these fields the researcher, not knowing beforehand what he is going to find, must be alive to each and every clue he comes across, any one of which could lead to some vital discovery that could bring his work to life in an exciting and original way.

In general, an article or thesis will require either factual or historical research, or both, whereas most books will demand a mixture of all three types of research, in varying proportions according to their subject and what the writer already knows. In a biography, for example, some factual research will be necessary to substantiate a quotation from a letter or diary of a certain date; historical research to fill in the detail of an event in which the subject of the biography played a leading part; background research to permit the author to describe, say, the environment in which that person grew up. In an historical novel, dates and names and events must be factually correct, while background research will be important in order to bring it to life, to add accurate details of costume, food, manners, etc. of the relevant period. In a modern short story or play, the setting must be authentic and the characters must speak the right language (slang, dialect or technical idiom related to their occupations and age). Some of the problems and pitfalls, as well as the sources of information appropriate to each of these categories of research, are outlined in later sections of this book.

Whatever the subject or nature of the search, the procedure is roughly the same. You may begin with one solid fact or several – this may be a date, or an event, or a name, or just an idea – and you build up your dossier rather like the CID officer tracks his criminal: with patience, persistence and, hopefully, the occasional lucky break. It may take you months to ferret out one vital clue, or you may chance upon it almost immediately; often, however, it is just when you have returned wearily to square one from yet another in a series of blind alleys that you stumble on the missing link (and curse yourself for following up so many red herrings on the way). All researchers know the elation this unexpected discovery produces, and it is nowhere more aptly described than by the university professor quoted in Dr A. L. Rowse's *A Cornish Childhood* as saying, '... I felt that curious thrill, the authentic sensation of the researcher ... It is as if you were to sit down and find you have sat on the cat. The thing comes alive in your hand . . .'. Peter Fleming, discussing the art of research with the late Joan St George Saunders of Writers' and Speakers' Research, the first professional research service in this country (there are several others now), likened it to fox hunting: 'The horns sound, one races for the first covert – then a halt while the hounds snuffle around in the undergrowth. Here the cunning hunter circles around the wood and knows instinctively which way the hounds will break. Off you go again and by the end of the day you are still there – perhaps to be blooded with success!'*

One of the researcher's greatest problems lies in deciding when to call it a day. It is always possible – and tempting – to go on delving just a little further – provided, of course, that time and adequate funds are available. But he must keep in mind the terms of reference of his work and discipline himself accordingly. Only experience will enable him to acquire the 'feel' of the job, to know when he should follow his hunch and go off at a tangent, when to replace the reference books on the shelf and pick up his pen. The temptation will nearly always be there to continue researching 'for a little while longer'. All too easily the writer can slip into the comfortable routine of a perpetual student.

It is a bad thing to postpone indefinitely the real creative process. Indeed, to prolong researching unduly is regarded by some historians as an indication of a fear of the actual writing. Therefore once a certain stage in the research has been reached, it is best to press on with a first draft. A modest amount of further research will almost certainly be necessary, and possible, at a later stage, when you will know more precisely what you need or in order to up-date, to fill in any gaps or to explore aspects of your subject which you may have ignored at the outset but now wish to include. Very often an editor or agent, after a first reading of the author's typescript, will suggest modifications or additions; in the case of a book, it will be the copy editor who will query with the author certain spellings or statements, some of which may involve extra research.

Modern society is constantly on the move, new studies appear every week, and since it now takes an average of between six and nine months from delivery of manuscript to the date of publication of a book, unless a writer is submitting an article of topical interest for almost instant publication in a newspaper or journal, it will be impossible for his work to be fully up-to-date. The current practice of going straight into page proofs instead of first into galleys and then

---

*Letter to the author from Mrs St George Saunders, 15 August 1975. Quoted by kind permission of Sir Alan Urwick.

into page has rendered it virtually impossible to make any but essential corrections and up-datings at this stage. You should not allow this to worry you unduly: it is the same for everyone, and a well researched, well written work will always achieve recognition as such.

In the fulfilment of his work, whether it be long or short, fiction or non-fiction, the author will surely have experienced the deep sense of satisfaction that is the reward of a thorough job of research. If it has not been altogether too traumatic an exercise, he may even go along with the view of the poet Robert Herrick:

> Attempt the end, and never stand to doubt;
> Nothing's so hard but search will find it out.

2

Organization and Method

The writer's first task, when embarking on a new project, is to survey and organize the material already in his possession. By the time he has done this, he will have a pretty good idea of how much additional research needs to be done. Then, and only then – and always bearing in mind the intended length and complexity of the end-product, as well as the time and funds available – is he ready to move on to tap other sources.

At this stage he should make a preliminary list of everything he needs to find out and where he thinks he will have to go to get it. The key here is to *plan ahead*. Books you want may be in use by other readers, so that you will have to wait a few weeks for them; the people you hope to interview may be busy or away; information you send for may take longer than you anticipate to arrive. You will be surprised also at how much time and money you will save by taking the trouble to write down all those people and places you envisage having to visit: with the aid of a good map and gazetteer you can plan itineraries that take in several assignments on each trip.

Just as it is false economy either to skip the amount of time necessary for a thorough study of basic material and sources, so it is foolish to neglect to give proper thought to setting up a system for the storage and easy retrieval of that material, remembering always to make suitable provision for material still to be acquired. Since both these operations cost money as well as time (time = money being a constant theme throughout this book), this is an appropriate place in which to outline some of the financial aspects of research.

Costs of Research

The first thing to remember is that it is always going to cost more than you expect. Leaving aside the question of working time, outgoings will include stationery and equipment, travelling and motor expenses, search fees (charged by some private libraries and by clergy in the case of parish registers), the purchase of books, periodicals and newspapers, photocopying, photography, telephone and postal expenses (these can be unexpectedly heavy). Meals away from home when researching can be expensive, and you should not forget the lighting, heating and cleaning of a room used as office or study, since over the years this too can mount up – and if you are making an income from writing most of such outgoings can be included as legitimate expenses to set against tax. The fees of a professional researcher, if employed, will be another major item, as will those of an indexer, and, at the end of the day, unless you are a good typist, you should allow for the cost of producing the final typescript in two or more copies. Computer-owners will need to calculate for the cost of the print-out from disk.

It is an excellent idea to make a list of every conceivable expense you think you are going to incur – and then double it. Costs are rising all the time, and if a book takes four years to complete instead of the eighteen months you envisaged at the outset, this will play havoc with your budget. However, you will not have to fork out the total amount in one go, but as you proceed.

If you are fortunate enough to have a book or article commissioned, explain to the publisher or editor before you negotiate the contract or settle the fee just how much research expenditure is likely to be involved, and, in the case of a book, try to negotiate an adequate advance against royalties; this will probably be payable in instalments. Journalists may be able to arrange their assignments on an expenses-paid basis. In all cases, it is wise to keep a record of every item of expenditure, from a packet of paper clips to the hotel bill, and to ask for receipts for all major payments: you may not be a published writer when you start out, but if you end up as the author of a bestseller or even a writer with a modest regular income from his work, you will need to justify your expenses to the tax inspector.

It is always dangerous to state prices in print, especially in these days of inflation. As a guideline to the uninitiated, however, it should be borne in mind that at the time of going to press (late summer 1985) professional researchers and indexers are charging between £7 and £15 an hour, and typists around £5 to £6 an hour. A ream of good quality typing paper retails at approximately £6 (for bond) or £4 (for bank); carbons cost £11.50 per 100; typewriter ribbons about £1.50. (If you shop around, you may be able to find a discount supplier selling these items at a lower price.) Servicing a typewriter will run into at least £20 or £30 a year. Photocopying varies from as little as 8p to 15p a sheet, depending on size (the cheapest being on coin-operated machines on which you make your own copies), to as much as 50p a sheet plus VAT for copies of newspaper pages (applications for these by post are subject to a minimum charge and handling fee). Genealogists and family historians are constantly bemoaning the fact that photocopies of birth, marriage and death certificates now cost £5 apiece (£10 by post).

One major expense so often overlooked by a writer is the cost of quoting from copyright material: fees are liable to be charged for anything more than a few lines, although in practice some agents and publishers will be content, in the case of a short passage, with a suitable acknowledgment or possibly a free copy of the book. Reproduction fees for illustrative material, on the other hand, vary according to the size of the reproduction and the nature of the rights sought (i.e. British Commonwealth rights, world rights etc.), but are normally not payable until the date of publication. Sometimes a publisher is willing to bear all or part of such expenses, and an author wishing to quote extensively from copyright material or to use pictures from private photographers, picture agencies or libraries would be well advised to ascertain the costs in advance and to discuss the financial division of responsibilities prior to the contract being drawn up for signature.

'Hidden' expenses will include the number of free copies an author is expected to hand out. Normally he will receive six free copies of his book and may buy additional copies at a substantial discount. It is courteous to give signed copies to those who have helped to prepare the book for the press, such as the professional researcher, translator, indexer or proof-reader (where these are not taken care of by the publisher), and to the typist; copies should also be presented to anyone who has provided a substantial amount of material or given the author access to private papers. The publisher is responsible for sending out review copies.

Equipment

No one would dream of taking up a sports or leisure activity without the proper equipment; nor should a writer or journalist embark on his researches lacking the few essential tools of the trade. It is true that pen and paper, the rudiments of shorthand or speed-writing, access to a good library, and an unlimited amount of time were once all that was needed, and although one might still 'get by' with these – today, when time is money (a recurrent theme of this book, for which I make no apology) – it is both sensible and practical to make full use of all that modern technology provides to help us obtain the information we seek as speedily and as inexpensively as possible.

Leaving aside micro-computers, microfilm and microfiche readers, which are dealt with below in a separate section, the basic equipment required can be divided into three groups: 1) equipment for use in the writer's study; 2) the tools he takes with him in briefcase or car when researching outside the home; and 3) equipment that is 'desirable' (i.e. where funds permit) or for special assignments.

The suggested items are (excluding normal stationery):

For the study
Typewriter
Good desk lamp
Tape recorder (or transcribing system) with foot pedal
Filing cabinet or other storage system
Card index system
Large magnifying glass
Stapler/punch (better than paper clips for fastening papers)
Paper guillotine (for trimming notes and enabling you to use all blank scraps)
Letter scales (will save a lot of time queuing at post office, especially if you keep a supply of stamps of varying denominations)
Highlighter pens in different colours (marvellous for marking up press cuttings/photocopies/notes)
Soft pencils (for writing on backs of photographs)

To take out 'on the job'
Briefcase and/or shoulder bag
Mini tape recorder/pocket memo, with plenty of spare cassettes and batteries
Larger tape recorder, with detachable microphone (for interviews)
Camera and plenty of film, flashbulbs, spare battery (if job requires it; Polaroid or disc camera would be adequate if pictures needed only for research purposes, but a good SLR at least is necessary if illustrating own work)
Clipboard (useful for writing on as you walk around or when interviewing)
Pocket magnifier
Mini-stapler
Phonecard (useful for making calls from phone boxes)
Plenty of biros *and* pencils (local record offices and most MSS departments of libraries permit note-taking only in pencil)
Ruler
Map of area to be visited
Local bus/rail time-tables
Small cash book (for noting all expenses)
Spare pair of reading glasses (if used)

For professional researchers or those with special assignments:
A more sophisticated tape recorder, such as those widely used by
    radio reporters (a 'must' if recordings are to be broadcast)
Telephone answering machine (to answer calls when you are out
    on the job)
Video recorder or clock radio/cassette recorder
Telephone charge clock (worth its weight in gold if you are on
    expenses, as you can read off costs of all calls instantly)

and, finally, for those who can afford them:

Computer with appropriate software, floppy and hard disks
Daisy wheel printer
Microfilm/microfiche reader
Photocopier

Computers

It does not fall within the scope of this book to discuss the pros and
cons of word-processing for writers. Any reader who is toying with
the idea of making such an investment, or indeed anyone interested
in the subject, would do well to read Ray Hammond's *The Writer
and the Word Processor* (Coronet Books, Hodder & Stoughton,
1984). But beware! The author will almost certainly convince you
that you do need one! (He will even tell you how to do it on a
shoestring.)

What *is* relevant here – and of paramount importance to the
modern researcher – is the use of the personal computer not only for
the storage and retrieval of research material, but also for 'on-line'
access to outside data-bases.

Storage of information on computer can be effected in one of three
ways. The cheapest is to use an ordinary audio cassette recorder, but
the recall of material thus stored is painfully slow by comparison to
the 'floppy' or 'hard' disk systems. A floppy disk system (preferably
one with a second disk drive) will probably be adequate for the
average writer/researcher; but the writer or professional researcher
embarking on a major research programme or wishing to establish
his own data-bank of source material will sooner rather than later
find it worthwhile to switch to a hard disk (also known as a
'Winchester') system, which is capable of storing up to a hundred
times the amount of data and which will produce the information
required on screen ten times faster. It is, of course, more expensive.

Going 'on-line' makes it possible for you, through your personal
computer, to communicate with other computers and so to extract

information from data-bases and data-banks all over the world. The only additional equipment that this involves is a 'modem' (which is plugged into the telephone) and some communications software; you then subscribe to one or more data-bases and on top of this you pay only for the time you are linked to the relevant data-base. Since the transmission of data via telecommunication channels is considerably cheaper than the cost of voice transmission (telephone calls) from one side of the globe to another, 'on-line' retrieval will cost you very much less than you might imagine. This is not to say, of course, that it is cheap. But it is only when you relate the cost to the vast wealth of material to which you have virtually instant access, and compare this with the amount of research that would be necessary, in terms of time = money, to give approximately the same result, that you come to appreciate its tremendous value and potential.

While it is unlikely that any but the established, prolific writer or the professional researcher will contemplate going 'on-line' at present, it should not be forgotten that access to a number of data-bases is available to individual members of the public through various library computer search services. (Details of BLAISE-LINE, the service offered by the British Library, will be found on page 35.) Whether or not an individual should go 'on-line' depends (a) on how much research he does and (b) on the value he puts on his personal working time. Most readers of this handbook will find it sufficient to use the library computer search service from time to time. For those who wish to know more about the subject, two books (among many) are highly recommended: Ray Hammond's *On-Line Handbook* (Fontana Paperback, 1984) and *Online Bibliographic Databases: A Directory and Sourcebook* by James L. Hall and Marjorie J. Brown (London: Aslib, 1983).

Microfilm/microfiche readers

It may not be many years before the micro-computer, microfilm and microfiche reader become as normal pieces of equipment in the writer's study as the typewriter is today: one has only to consider the dramatic increase in filmed material in recent years, and the space-saving advantages the storage of filmed material has over printed and bound books, to see that this is a real possibility. Until the day comes when we are borrowing almost as many microfilms as books from the library, however, it will scarely be economic to purchase such a machine for private use. The writer needing to study microfilms at home on a short-term basis may be able to find a firm who will hire him a machine for this purpose (consult the yellow pages of your local telephone directory, or write to one of the big photographic firms such as Kodak, Bell & Howell or 3M; alternatively you can ask the Microfilm Association of Great Britain, Dellfield, Pednor, Chesham, Bucks HP5 2SX).

Photocopiers

Unless a writer does a great deal of photocopying, it is hardly worthwhile purchasing a machine. Some of the cheaper desk-top models will copy only from loose sheets and on special (expensive) paper, and not all those that will take bound books give satisfactory results, especially if the volume to be copied is thick and tightly bound. Although eager salesmen may promise copies at a fraction of the commercial cost, which can be tempting, when one takes into account the cost of materials, electricity, servicing charges, annual depreciation of the machine and operating time – valuable working time – there is not that much saving. The prime value of having a photocopier at hand is the *convenience* of being able to run off copies instantly, without making a special trip to town.

Organization of Material

There are few hard and fast rules in research, but it is wise to establish at the outset, and adhere to, some systematic method of note-taking and storage of data. There is little point in accumulating a mass of notes, press cuttings and other material unless a system is devised whereby you are able to pull out reasonably quickly what you want when you want it in the course of writing. It is equally important that you should replace that material after use in such a way that you can put your hands on it instantly at a later date.

Methods may differ according to individual circumstances and taste, and according to the type of documentation to be handled. The researcher who is already geared to a computer will feed his research into his personal data-bank, either on 'floppy' or 'hard' disk. The rest of us fall into two camps – those who favour a card index system, and those who prefer notebooks, pads or sheets of paper, with a cabinet large enough to house them.

Card index system

The great advantage of a card index is its flexibility. It need not be expensive if slips of paper cut to the correct size are used instead of cards (a local printer will often supply these, using offcuts from other jobs, at a very low cost) and, for further economy, old envelope cartons, shoe boxes, cereal packets or similar containers can be cut down and converted into temporary filing receptacles, suitably labelled, and using stiff card to make alphabetical or other guide cards for the necessary divisions. For more permanent use the commercially manufactured metal or plastic index boxes or drawers are recommended; guide cards with plastic tabs are the most hard-wearing, and record cards will stand up to continual handling better than the flimsier slips. (For real economy, the researcher can always do what some professional indexers do, and once a particular job is finished, re-use the cards or slips by writing on the other side – preferably using a different coloured biro so that there is no danger of confusion should the odd one be accidentally turned over.)

Cards or slips may be carried to and from the reference library or other place of research, as required, either in envelopes (clearly marked in subjects or whatever divisions best fit the job in hand) or in small packs secured by rubber bands. They can be sorted into alphabetical, subject or chronological order, either in one continuous series or per chapter and, if necessary, re-grouped as the work proceeds; coloured cards and coloured stickers (available in various shapes) may be used to denote different subjects or periods within each main division, and slips bearing brief cross-references can be inserted as appropriate. The value of such a system is that its permutations are so great.

Loose sheets and notebooks

Many writers prefer to make their notes on larger sheets of paper. For them the shorthand reporter type of notebook is to be recommended, or there are various sizes of ruled pads, with or without punched holes for fitting into loose-leaf ring binders or spring binders. Keeping notes in exercise books is not a good idea, unless a separate book is used for each section of the research, and even then it is advisable to number the pages and make a simple index in the front of the book, otherwise it may be difficult to locate the exact subject-matter when it is required.

For filing purposes it is best, when using sheets of paper rather than cards or slips, to note each item on a separate sheet or at least to leave a good gap between each item so that the notes can be cut up at home and each one slotted individually into its right folder or envelope. Although this may sound extravagant, writing on both sides of the sheet, unless it is on the same subject and clearly indicated by a bold 'PTO' or arrow at the bottom right-hand corner of the first side, is false economy – much valuable material has been 'lost' in this way. It is all too easy to gather up notes and file them without checking to see what is written on the back; nothing is more frustrating to the writer than to *know* that he has made a note of some vital fact or quotation or source – but *where*? It is also a good plan to get into the habit of putting material away as soon as possible after returning from the library, or after use. Otherwise the telephone may ring, there is nothing else handy on which to jot down a message, so the sheets lying on the desk are turned over, scribbled on – inevitably, sooner or later, something will go astray.

Working chronologies

Some writers engaged on an historical study or biography find it helpful to make themselves a working chronology to keep at their elbow while they work. This can be a straightforward listing of events or, in the case of a biography, may consist of a loose-leaf ring binder with the sheets arranged so that when the book is open the left-hand page lists the happenings in the life of the biographee and his family, while the right-hand page lists outside events of approximately the same date. Ample space should be left between dates for subsequent insertions as research proceeds, to avoid the necessity of retyping pages. The time spent on the preparation of this simple working tool will be amply repaid by the ease with which the writer will be able to see his subject in perspective as he works.

Another useful system for the non-fiction writer is a small card index containing, on separate cards, a brief note of all the important points that must be covered, chapter by chapter. Before planning each chapter the writer can cast his eye over the cards and re-group them in the order in which he intends to deal with them, and when that chapter is finished anything that needs to be mentioned again later can be transferred on to the relevant section, so that he will not lose sight of it when the time comes.

Filing

If the documentation is not vast, the most convenient form of storage may be in large manila envelopes, clear plastic or multi-coloured document wallets, numbered or clearly marked as to subject or content; some researchers prefer the 'concertina' type of file or the folders secured with elastic that have up to nine divisions. For all but the simplest research collections, however, a steel filing cabinet will be a worthwhile investment. There are some small trolley-type cabinets on castors, which will suit the writer who likes to have his material at his elbow, at desk or armchair, wherever he works; otherwise the single, 2-, 3- or 4-drawer cabinet, with or without suspension filing, is the best buy. As each book or writing project is completed, the material can be cleared out, parcelled up and stored elsewhere to make space for the next assignment.

So far as the storage of used material is concerned, the cardboard cartons obtainable free from wine shops and supermarkets are most useful; but photographs and manuscripts are best kept dust-free and flat in the boxes usually supplied with most good quality typing papers. For the perfectionist, or the writer who envisages the need to have quick access to his old material, there are on the market excellent lightweight storage containers, ranging from collapsible box files to the more rigid corrugated board storage cabinet complete with drawers. It is worth remembering that cardboard allows documents to 'breathe', whereas metal does not; valuable archive material (e.g. original letters) should not be kept for any length of time in a closed filing cabinet.

Whatever system is adopted, and it will vary according to individual needs (and pockets), there are two essentials that will prove their worth over and over again: the establishment of a key for quick reference, and a system of clear labelling. Notebooks with alphabetical divisions or the most compact of desk-top card indexes are adequate for the former, a supply of labels and felt marker pens in various colours for the latter. The card index, which may be kept in a box or in a rotary filing unit, should be as simple as possible, containing just sufficient information – either names and telephone numbers, or titles of books and periodicals, with page references and/or dates, or any suitable code of reference numbers – to send the user directly to the required source material.

A word of advice now to those who are setting up a new filing system – THINK BIG! As work progresses, you are bound to accumulate at least twice as much material as you planned for, and you should bear in mind, too, that a 4-drawer filing cabinet takes up no more floor space than the single-drawer model. Few writers will be like the well-known historian and biographer who has admitted to having taken four years to decide to buy a proper filing cabinet and another four years to fill it – but those who do find themselves with empty drawers at the outset can always put them to good use. (Think of the peace of mind it will give you when you go away to research or on holiday to know that the one and only copy of your unfinished manuscript is securely stowed away, comparatively fireproof and out of the reach of vandals!)

The same goes for original material loaned to the writer. This is a big responsibility, and it is advisable always to make a point of photocopying or taking notes of what you need and returning the originals to their owners without delay. If this is absolutely not possible, at least keep the material in a safe place. Newspaper cuttings will go brown if kept in the daylight for any length of time, photographs can be easily damaged and rendered unsuitable for reproduction if left lying around on the desk, and some picture agencies require the borrower to pay substantial costs for the loss or damage of negatives or transparencies.

Books should always be treated with special care, whether they are loaned by private individuals or borrowed from the library. If they are to be handled a great deal, it is a good idea to cover them with plastic film or brown paper. *Never* write in the margins or turn down corners to mark a reference (unless of course the book belongs to you and you regard it as a working copy); and be very careful when photocopying that you do not bend it in such a way as to damage the binding.

Take special care only to write on the backs of photographs with a very soft pencil; anything else can do irreparable damage. It is best to keep all illustrative material in a separate drawer, box file or filing tray, with each print inside a plastic folder or stiffened envelope. Elementary advice, maybe, but it is a fact that many photographs suffer through being left lying about unprotected; even if they are stacked underneath other papers they may sometimes inadvertently be scribbled on, and once that kind of damage is done it cannot be undone.

For those who are interested, there is an excellent British Museum publication, *Caring for Books and Documents* by A. D. Baynes-Cope (latest reprint 1982). Researchers who handle original documents are also recommended to read 'Notes on the Use of Private Papers for Historical Research' in the *Bulletin of the Institute of Historical Research*, November 1966 (reprints of this useful article are available from the Royal Commission on Historical Manuscripts, Quality House, Quality Court, Chancery Lane, London WC2A 1HP).

Three final tips:

1 Having set up the system that suits you and your project, do make an effort to keep the filing up to date, or the whole purpose will be defeated. If it is not possible to slot material away as it comes in, it is a good idea to keep some kind of 'pending' box or file, or a nest of filing baskets, into which you can put it until you have the time.
2 Remember that every good filing system has a 'Miscellaneous' file, and get into the habit of looking there for anything you cannot find instantly. As the 'Miscellaneous' file grows — and it is wise to allow plenty of space for it — new subject headings will suggest

themselves and the appropriate material can be extracted and filed separately.

3 NEVER THROW AWAY ANY NOTES without keeping a record of the sources.

Research Methods

Having established his storage system, the writer is ready to go out and seek the additional material he needs.

Use of libraries

Finding your way round the library or libraries where you intend to do the bulk of your research is half the battle for the writer. The first thing to remember is that the librarian's job is to guide the researcher or reader to the right books; he or she is not paid to do their original research for you. It is nevertheless astonishing how much a cooperative, interested librarian *will* do, and it is always politic to take him into your confidence about the scope of your research and what you are writing. Similarly, it is advisable to contact the librarian of a special library, either by telephone or letter, before making a first visit; provided he is given due notice of your interest, the librarian or one of his assistants will usually then prepare a preliminary selection of titles, and work can begin without delay. If you do not do this, you may find that the librarians are tied up with other readers when you arrive, and you can easily waste half a day of valuable researching time.

In public libraries, the reference departments of most public libraries, and the majority of special and private subscription libraries, the reader has access to the stacks and will be free to browse among the books arranged on the shelves related to his subject; where this is not the case, he should ask a library assistant to explain how the catalogue or subject index is arranged and how to order books. At the major university libraries and the British Library, a certain number of reference works are on the so-called 'open shelves', but all other titles must be applied for on the library requisition slips; this involves looking up the relevant shelf-marks in the general catalogue. As it may be anything up to two hours before the books are delivered to the reader's desk, it is essential to order what is needed at the earliest moment, if not a day or two in advance, and to fill in the waiting period by using works that are on the open shelves or by looking up shelf marks of books that you are going to need in the next phase of your research. Because of lack of space, many libraries today 'out-house' selected classes of books; for example, some British Library titles are kept in a depository at Woolwich and may take 24 hours or more to arrive at the Bloomsbury reading room.

Researchers wishing to use the British Library or other copyright libraries, those of the Imperial War Museum, National Maritime Museum, Royal Botanical Gardens and most university and museum libraries must obtain a reader's ticket, and it is advisable to do so in advance of your first visit – although temporary day tickets will usually be issued on demand. Applications have to be countersigned by someone of authority (a JP, doctor or person of recognised professional status) who will vouch for you as a responsible person; you will also be asked to state the nature of your research. There is no charge, and tickets once obtained are normally renewable, but intending readers are required to state in the first instance that they cannot undertake their particular research in other libraries. Write to the Director of the relevant library for full details and application forms.

On your first visit to a library, you will need to devote a little time to familiarising yourself with the layout and cataloguing system. Ask one of the library assistants to explain any unusual features, and how to look up anonymous works, year books and directories, or the proceedings of learned societies. Some major libraries display a map showing the layout, or there may be a printed leaflet available. Most have separate card indexes arranged under authors and subjects, but occasionally one comes across a 'dictionary' type of catalogue which combines author, subject and title in one alphabetical listing. Nowadays the catalogue after a certain date is most likely to be on microfiche or cassette; the updating of these by computer is a godsend to researchers, as it keeps the listings constantly up to date.

In smaller libraries the catalogue is usually cumulative, but in others there may be separate drawers or cabinets containing cards for acquisitions within a stated period. This 'Recent Acquisitions' section should not be overlooked. The trap here for the inexperienced lies in the word 'acquisitions', for although this section of the catalogue will comprise mainly new titles, it will also include books that have been purchased or otherwise acquired recently – some of which may have been published a number of years ago. When you fail to find the book you are looking for in the general catalogue, therefore, always turn to this section.

The majority of libraries in the United Kingdom have adopted the Dewey Decimal Classification, which divides human knowledge into ten classes, each sub-divided to accommodate subjects within each class. The researcher should try to memorise the main divisions, as follows:

000	General Works
100	Philosophy
200	Religion
300	Social Sciences
400	Languages
500	Science
600	Technology
700	The Arts and Recreations
800	Literature
900	Geography, Biography and History

The *British National Bibliography (BNB)* also uses the Dewey classification, and if you are seeking a published work on a certain subject, and do not know the author or precise title, you should go straight to the relevant class listing, as you would do in the library.

Note-taking

There are three 'golden rules' of researching:

1 *Copy accurately*
   Care must be taken to retain original spellings in quoted matter, using an editorial *sic* in square brackets if necessary. It is a good idea to get into the habit of double-checking all figures and proper names immediately they are written or typed. '1943' can so easily be copied as '1934' when one is tired (or more easily, because one's mind is on the current date, '1968' as '1986'!), and whereas it takes only a few seconds to verify the figure at the time, such a mistake can take hours to correct later – or may not be discovered until the work is in print. Writing unusual proper names and place names in block capitals in the researcher's notes also helps to avoid error and will save a lot of trouble if, several weeks later, the writer is unable to decipher his own hurried scribbles.
2 *Check, double-check and, if in doubt, triple-check all facts*
   Primarily where verbal recollections are given to the researcher by private individuals, but whenever and wherever possible in all other cases, especially if any doubts are entertained as to the accuracy of facts (even if printed facts), these should be verified in another source. Where confirmation of a fact or figure cannot be obtained and the writer remains in doubt, it is best either to avoid using it or, if you must, to state the source or sources relied on. The

problem of 'conflicting authorities' is discussed in the section on Historical Research (page 61).

3 *Keep a note of all sources*

The importance of keeping full reference notes cannot be over-stressed. Valuable time may be wasted if, for example, when his first draft is written, the writer wishes to examine a particular source in more detail but cannot turn up instantly a note of the author, title, date and relevant page number, and preferably also the shelf-mark of the library where he originally saw it. Even more time will be wasted if he has omitted to follow the recommendation under (1) above to check his page references at the time and, failing to find what he is looking for at, say, page 241, he has to thumb through a hefty tome, possibly without the help of an index, only to discover the right passage at page 421. (Whenever this happens, the short-cut is to try first all the permutations for the number originally writen down.) Making brief cards or slips for each reference as you go along will halve the work when it comes to compiling a 'notes and references' section or the bibliography (see the section on Preparation for the Press, pages 141-9). Press cuttings and photocopies should be clearly marked with the book title, newspaper or periodical, plus volume number, date, publisher and page number where appropriate.

Photocopying

All reference libraries and most other libraries and record offices operate a photocopy service, subject to the usual copyright restrictions and a ban on old or rare editions that might be damaged in the process. Microfilms and the type of photocopy suitable for reproduction can usually be obtained only from major libraries and record offices, and may take several weeks, but the electrostatic print or 'rapid copy' or 'xerox' as it is sometimes called, which is the most useful to the researcher, is often available while you wait or within 24 hours. Some libraries have coin-operated machines installed and expect you to make your own copies.

With material that is out of copyright there is no problem, but unless the copyright owner has given permission in writing, copying of all other printed matter is restricted to one article from any one issue of a newspaper or periodical, at any one time; or to one single extract of up to 4,000 words, or a series of extracts none of which exceeds 3,000 words, up to a total of 8,000 words, or one-tenth of any one book in copyright. In all cases the researcher will be required to sign a statement that he requires the photocopies for the purposes of research or private study. The cost is modest when one considers the amount of time it takes to copy a text by hand. Another factor to be borne in mind is that the photocopy is an *accurate* copy. When ordering photocopies from a library, it is essential to keep a note of the author, title, date of publication and edition of the source material, since these will not always appear on the photocopied sheets and the originals may not be returned to you; write these on the photocopies before storing.

Commercial photocopying services abound in every city and major town these days, with self-operating machines at some railway stations, department stores and supermarkets. The quality of copies varies considerably, as does the cost; some places offer a substantial discount for a large number of copies made at any one time. These 'copy shops' are not usually worried about copyright and will often copy a complete book without demur, although in so doing both they and the purchaser are breaking the law. Anyone planning to copy a large amount of text still in copyright should first apply for permission to the publisher.

Infringement of copyright by reprography is an international problem. At the time of going to press (late summer 1985) negotiations are in progress for the establishment of a licensing scheme for the reprographic reproduction and duplication of texts; the British Copyright Council (Copyright House, 29-33 Berners Street, London W1P 4AA) has issued a booklet on the subject, *Reprographic Copying of Copyright Books and Journals.*

Copyright

A writer wishing to quote substantially from a work in copyright – which in the United Kingdom lasts during an author's lifetime and for fifty years after his death – must obtain permission from the copyright owner. This will normally be the writer of the work in question, if he is still alive, or his heirs and/or literary executor or anyone to whom he may have assigned the copyright after his death. It sometimes takes quite a while to trace the copyright owner, and it is prudent therefore to make application to use such material in good time, through the original publisher of the relevant work. Biographers and historians should remember that although a letter *belongs* to the recipient, the copyright in it is vested in the writer of the letter and, after his death, to his estate; this applies also to letters published in the press.

British copyright law is immensely complicated. While the quotation of short passages for the purposes of criticism or review is deemed to be 'fair dealing', in all other cases involving more than a short phrase or a couple of lines of poetry it is advisable to seek permission. Some publishers hold that quotations totalling less than

400 words from any one work do not require special clearance, provided that acknowledgment is made to the author, title and publisher; but most literary agents and the Society of Authors recommend formal clearance. A fee will sometimes be payable, the amount depending on the length of the passage or passages it is intended to quote and on the nature of the rights sought (i.e. British only, or British Commonwealth or world rights). Foreign rights are frequently controlled by publishers or literary agents abroad, but the UK publisher should be able to provide a name and address to write to. It is most important to allow adequate time for the clearance of all such requests before going to press.

International copyright is safeguarded by two separate conventions: the Berne Convention and the Universal Copyright Convention, to which different countries adhere. For details of these and of the new Copyright Statute of the United States, which came into force in January 1978, see the articles on British and US copyright in the current *Writers' & Artists' Yearbook*.

In the United Kingdom a White Paper on copyright reform is due out towards the end of 1985. Meanwhile the most up-to-date work on the subject is the second edition of J. M. Cavendish's *Handbook of British Publishing Practice* (Cassell, London 1984). The Society of Authors (84 Drayton Gardens, London SW10 9SD) publishes a useful *Quick Guide* on copyright, which is free to members and available to non-members at £1 post free. See also *Copyright* by Christopher Scarles, in the *Authors' and Printers' Guides* series published by Cambridge University Press.

Use of typewriters, tape recorders and other mechanical aids

Some major libraries have special typing rooms for students or set aside a portion of one search room for those who wish to bring typewriters. This is a useful facility where there is a long delay in photocopying, as the researcher can take home with him at the end of the day everything he has copied. The number of microfilm, cassette or microfiche readers is often limited, and if you know in advance that the records to be consulted are on film or tape or fiche it is wise to enquire whether advance notice should be given of an intended visit. Portable tape recorders are not usually permissible, except by special arrangement with the librarian – this will depend on whether or not a private room can be made available so that other readers are not disturbed. Dictating into a tape recorder undoubtedly saves time and fatigue, in the library, but can create problems of transcription unless proper names are spelled out and punctuation indicated; nothing at all will be saved if, at the end of the day, it proves necessary to go back to the original to check a quotation. The researcher will find a small tape recorder of real value, however, where a good deal of interviewing or travelling has to be done: even if there are objections to using such a device during an interview, a quick dash to the car or hotel afterwards to record one's impressions while all is fresh in one's mind is very worthwhile, and so is a recorded on-the-spot description of buildings and scenes to be portrayed in a writer's work. For this purpose the small battery-operated type of machine known as a 'pocket memo' or 'electronic notebook' is ideal, as it is hand-held. A larger machine with separate microphone and facility for longer-playing tapes is more suitable for interviewing, and here it is best to choose a model which will run both on batteries and on mains. The latter will probably have a socket for plugging in a foot pedal (essential for tape transcription); if you intend to transcribe much of the material on your mini-cassettes, then you will need a transcriber (again with foot pedal).

Using a modern clock radio-cum-cassette recorder or television video recorder it is possible to record programmes from radio or TV while you are away from home, and this too can be of value to the researcher who must be elsewhere when such programmes are on air or screen.

It may be opportune here to pass on a few hints on the use of microfilm readers. The machines do vary slightly, and it is wise in the first instance to ask a library assistant to show you how to operate one. It is very important never to touch the film with greasy fingers or to get it twisted, and always to re-wind the film onto the original spool before returning it to the issue desk. (Nothing is more exasperating to the next user than to discover that the spool must be re-wound!). In libraries where there are a number of machines installed, there is bound to be a good deal of noise as users wind and re-wind, and some people find they cannot do more than an hour or two's work on microfilm at a time, partly because of the noise and partly due to eyestrain. Some professional researchers surmount these difficulties with the aid of ear plugs and/or tinted glasses.

So far as using microfiches is concerned, you should always make a point of replacing the fiches in their correct slot after use (they are each numbered clearly in the top right-hand corner).

Interviewing

Interviewing people, and getting the maximum information out of them, is a skill that comes with practice. There are no hard and fast rules, but here are a few tips from personal experience:

26

Always write or telephone in advance, stating clearly who you are, why you need the information, and precisely what it is you seek.

If time permits, take 'two bites at the cherry'. People are naturally on the defensive at a first interview, but when you go back a second time they already know you and will welcome you as a 'friend'.

Don't ask a crucial or controversial question right at the start. If necessary, put the person being interviewed at ease, make some social small talk first. It can be quite productive sometimes to bring out your 'key' question almost at the end of the interview, as though it were an afterthought and not all that important – the interviewee will be relaxed by that time and much more expansive.

Don't assume that you can use a tape recorder. A lot of people are nervous of being recorded and will 'freeze' if you insist. A good plan is to have your machine tucked away in your briefcase and then, when the interview is well under way, you can say something like, 'This is tremendously good stuff, I can't get it all down accurately in my rusty shorthand... would you mind very much if I switched on my recorder?'

Always offer to let interviewees see anything you are going to quote in print, and ask them how they would wish to be acknowledged. And never fail to write afterwards to thank them for sparing the time to talk to you.

The question of how far to trust information given to you from personal recollection is dealt with in the chapter on Biography (see page 97).

A useful booklet, prepared primarily for the guidance of genealogists, or those compiling family or local histories, is Eve McLaughlin's *Interviewing Elderly Relatives*, published in 1985 by the Federation of Family History Societies (31, Seven Star Road, Solihull, West Midlands B91 2B2, price £1.10 including postage).

In the last decade modern technology has totally transformed the researcher's job, firstly by giving him access to source material in greater quantity and faster than ever before, and secondly by liberating him from the more irksome manual tasks that used to take up so much of his working time. Other technological 'miracles', some of which are already in the pipeline, will undoubtedly follow during the lifetime of this book. It will be up to the writers and researchers of the future to take full advantage of these innovations and to harness them to their particular needs as they arrive. Meanwhile the writer/researcher is still going to garner the bulk of his source material in the library or archives centre; the techniques of note-taking and interviewing, as described above, will continue to be practised; and the proper storage of research material will always be of special importance.

Postscript. As this handbook goes to press, a new book, written primarily for students preparing theses and writers of research reports, *Doing Your Own Research* by Eileen Kane, Marion Boyars Publishers, 1985, has appeared. It contains valuable advice on research methods, presentation and sources.

3

Basic Sources of Information and their Location

A writer's raw material will normally be derived from a combination of the following sources: personal knowledge, experience and observation; printed, microfilmed or computer-stored material (books, newspapers, periodicals, etc.); unpublished documentary, recorded or filmed sources (manuscripts, family papers, theses, archive collections, tapes, photographs, etc.); and other people's knowledge, experience and observation. Of these the most important must be the first-mentioned, since it is a writer's own viewpoint, drawn from his personal knowledge, experience and observation, that above all else puts a stamp of originality upon his work and distinguishes it from the work of every other writer.

Except where the work in hand is one of pure reminiscence – and even then certain statements will probably need to be substantiated by fact – it is however not enough to rely solely upon your own knowledge. As soon as your original material has been studied and sorted according to the shape of the projected piece of writing, you must consider what are the other sources of information to be tapped.

Printed Sources: Books

Printed books and information about books are obtainable primarily from bookshops, publishers and libraries. When you are engaged on a specific project, you will always find it worthwhile to acquire copies of the standard works on your subject, which you can keep at your elbow and either annotate in the margins or interleave with narrow strips of paper or markers on which you write some basic headings or other indications. It goes without saying that library books and books belonging to other people should *never* be marked in any way; but 'working copies' are a writer's essential reference tools and should be used to the best advantage.

New books may be purchased from booksellers or, in case of difficulty, direct from the publishers. A good bookseller will be aware of what has been published recently on a particular subject and, through *The Bookseller* and other trade papers, and his contact with publishers' representatives, of what is forthcoming. He will look up titles for a customer in the current *Books in Print*, *Paperbacks in Print* or *International Books in Print*, and in individual publishers' catalogues. If the title is not in stock, however, delivery may take a couple of weeks or more, depending on the publisher, and it is sometimes quicker to telephone one of the larger bookshops in London or one of the big provincial cities rather than wait for your local shop to obtain a copy.

A most useful and inexpensive publication for the book-buyer is Peter Marcan's *Directory of Specialist Bookdealers in the United Kingdom*, which lists bookshops under subject headings and contains a great deal of other relevant, practical information. Those who live in the south-east will find Diana Stephenson's *Bookshops of London* invaluable: as well as general and specialist booksellers, it includes details of antiquarian and secondhand dealers (with a subject index).

The bulk of the books you will need for your research are likely to come from libraries, and even recently published titles can be obtained reasonably quickly through the public library service if an application card is filled in at the time you see a book announced, or a review; this costs a few pence for reservation, and normally such new books may not be renewed after the initial 3-4 week borrowing period, if they are reserved by another reader. However, three weeks should be sufficient for you to make any notes you require, or to decide whether or not you need to purchase the book.

Provided you are not in a hurry, you should be able to obtain most of the books you need through the public library service, thanks to the inter-library lending scheme and the services of the British Library Lending Division at Boston Spa, West Yorkshire. Application to the Lending Division must be made either through the British Library or your local public library, not direct.

If you are unwilling to wait – and so often material is required for one chapter or section of your work before you can proceed to the next – it may be worth your while to travel to London or your nearest centre for a day or two's research in one of the copyright, university or other major reference libraries. It should be remembered, however, that new titles are not instantly available in such libraries: the acquisition and cataloguing processes may take up to a few months.

Copyright and reference libraries

Under the provisions of various Copyright Acts that have been passed since 1709, and of which the 1911 Act is still in force, certain libraries are entitled to receive one free copy of every book published in the United Kingdom. These are: the British Library (London); the Bodleian Library (Oxford); the Cambridge University Library (Cambridge); the National Library of Wales (Aberystwyth); the National Library of Scotland (Edinburgh); and Trinity College Library (Dublin).

In all these libraries the researcher can be confident of finding everything he needs that has been published from the 18th century onwards, and also much earlier material (collections that have been bequeathed or titles purchased over the years in the saleroom). A small percentage of stock may have been destroyed during the last war or otherwise mislaid.

Graduates and other *bona fide* researchers and students are able to use the various well-stocked university libraries, of which the University of London Library, the John Rylands University Library of Manchester and the Sydney Jones Library of Liverpool University are excellent examples. Other libraries include those of the major museums, such as (in London), the Imperial War Museum, the National Maritime Museum, the Natural History Museum, the Science Museum, and the Royal Botanical Gardens at Kew.

Major reference libraries open to the general public include the Central Reference Library just behind Trafalgar Square, London; Birmingham Central Reference Library; and Newcastle-upon-Tyne Central Library. A visit to the nearest of these and to other reference libraries in the provinces may well fulfil your needs and save you from the expense of travelling farther afield.

Admission to the British Library and other copyright and major libraries is free. Readers' tickets, valid for one or more years, are issued on personal application and are for research which cannot be done elsewhere (the subject of research must be stated and the form signed by a university tutor, a member of the legal profession or some other person of authority who will vouch for you as a responsible person). Tickets must be shown each time you enter the library; temporary tickets, valid for one or two days, will usually be issued on the spot without formality. Allow a little extra time on your first visit for this purpose: some libraries nowadays insist on taking an instant photograph for incorporation into the reader's ticket.

Holders of public library tickets in their home town may use them to borrow books from some of the lending branches of public

31

libraries in London; tickets may also be used at other libraries by arrangement with the librarian.

Many libraries are open late on certain evenings in the week. At the British Library, the Reading Room does not close until 9 p.m. on Tuesdays, Wednesdays and Thursdays; the Central Reference Library in Westminster is open until 7 p.m. from Monday to Friday. If you have to travel some distance, you would do well to plan your schedule to make the maximum use of the longest possible working day. Books usually have to be handed in half-an-hour before closing time, and photocopying orders will not be accepted after a certain time, so that it is important not only to allow for any necessary last-minute note-taking, but also for ordering, and paying for, photocopies.

For those who can afford it, a subscription to the London Library, 14 St James's Square, London SW1Y 4LG (tel. 01-930 7705), will prove very worthwhile. Members may take out ten books at a time (fifteen for country members, who may also borrow by post but have to pay the postage in both directions). Subscribers have access to the stacks, the use of a comfortable reading room and may purchase the printed author catalogue and subject index volumes (a boon to those who live in remote areas and wish to order by post or telephone). The annual subscription, currently £75, may be set against a professional writer's tax; short-term subscriptions are available, with or without borrowing facilities (apply to the Librarian for details).

Another London subscription library is the Highgate Literary and Scientific Library, 11 South Grove, Highgate Village, London N6 6BS (tel. 01-340 3343); the subscription there is £12 for one person, £18 for a family. In the provinces excellent subscription libraries exist in Leeds, Newcastle, Nottingham, Plymouth, and elsewhere.

Some special libraries make a small daily or half-daily charge for non-members and will occasionally lend books on payment of a deposit (refundable when the books are returned).

Special libraries

The use of libraries in general has been discussed in the previous chapter. The questions that now arise concern location: how to find out about the special libraries that are likely to help you in your particular field, and how to locate in those libraries the particular books you need.

The first place to look is in the *Aslib Directory of Information Sources in the United Kingdom*. This gives a comprehensive listing of practically every library and source of information in this country; it contains a subject index and details such as opening hours and the facilities available; it is brought up to date regularly, and all libraries possess the latest edition – ask for it at the enquiry desk. Other useful guides are the *Libraries, Museums and Art Galleries Year Book*, J. Burkett's *Library and Information Networks in the United Kingdom*, and the regional *Library Resources* series published by the Library Association Reference Special and Information Section.

The best international guides to libraries and research institutions are *The World of Learning*, H. Lengenfelder's *The World Guide to Libraries* and *The World Guide to Special Libraries*, while for Europe there are two other valuable reference works: *Subject Collections in European Libraries*, published by Bowker, containing 12,000 entries arranged under the Dewey Decimal Classification, and J. Burkett's *Library and Information Networks in W. Europe*.

Regrettably, space does not permit the mention in this handbook of more than a few individual libraries, named in the text under the various subjects of research discussed. A selective list of UK libraries is printed in Appendix 1 and of foreign libraries under the relevant country in chapter 9, 'Information from Foreign Sources'. The Library Association's *Libraries in the United Kingdom and the Republic of Ireland* is a handy annual paperback which lists addresses, telephone numbers and names of librarians.

Catalogues and guides

Every library has a catalogue of some kind, either an author index or a subject or title index, or all three, on cards or microfiche; some of the larger libraries have printed catalogues and guides to their collections, and these are usually available on the open shelves of the reference library. For the British Library, for example, there is, at one end of the scale, the 360-volume *General Catalogue of Printed Books to 1975* and, at the other, a useful little booklet, *British Library Reference Collections*.

It often happens, however, that you need information at the library on a subject about which you know very little, let alone the names of authors or titles of authoritative works, and here a subject index will not be of much help, as it will list only the relevant titles that are on the shelves of that particular library, and it will not evaluate them. There are several ways round this problem: to ask the reference librarian for the 'standard work' and for any recent studies, and evaluate them yourself (a glance at the index and bibliography will give a pretty good idea of how thoroughly an author has gone into his subject and how up-to-date the book is); to consult Walford's *Guide to Reference Material* or its US equivalent, Sheehy's *Guide to Reference Books*, published by the Library Association and the American Library Association respectively, the latter title being more international in outlook (both have excellent subject indexes); to read up the subject initially in a modern encyclopedia and use the short bibliography normally given there as a starting point for further research; or to use a more comprehensive bibliography where one exists. Gavin L. Higgens' *Printed Reference Material*, written for librarians, is highly recommended as a bibliography and evaluation of reference books for research: it should be on the bookshelf of every writer and professional researcher.

Bibliographies

The best way to find out if there is a bibliography on a certain subject is to consult the *World Bibliography of Bibliographies* and the cumulative *Bibliographic Index*, both of which should be available in most major libraries. Among special subject bibliographies likely to be of most use to the British writer/researcher are the *Bibliography of British Literary Bibliographies*; the *Handbook to County Bibliography*; the *London Bibliography of the Social Sciences*; and the *New Cambridge Bibliography of English Literature*. Recent UK titles can be traced in the *British National Bibliography*, known as the *BNB*, which has been published weekly since 1950, with regular cumulations and author, title and subject indexes. The bibliographies of other countries are listed in volume 3 of the *Guide to Reference Material* mentioned above, under 'National Bibliographies', and also in the UNESCO handbook, *Bibliographical Services throughout the World*. The *World Bibliographical Series* launched in 1977 by Clio Press aims to provide a uniform collection of bibliographies covering every country in the world, at the rate of about 15 volumes per year.

The Library Association, 7 Ridgmount Street, London WC1E 7AE (tel. 01-636 7543) has published bibliographies on a variety of subjects over the years, and these will be found in most reference libraries or in the Association's own library. It is also always worth enquiring from the Book Trust (formerly National Book League), Book House, 45 East Hill, Wandsworth, London SW18 2QZ (tel. 01-870 9055) whether they have a book list on a particular subject.

The British Library Science Reference Library (Holborn branch) will compile select bibliographies on specialised scientific and technological topics. Requests, with precise details of what is required, should be sent to the Deputy Director (Services), Science

Reference Library (SRL), 25 Southampton Buildings, Chancery Lane, London WC2A 1AW. The Library will also accept enquiries by telephone, telex or post for information on scientific and technological literature; and a computer search service is available. A reader's ticket is not necessary for those wishing to use the SRL.

Readers unfamiliar with bibliographic practice should remember that the numbers given in the index are entry numbers, *not* page numbers.

Book information services

The British Library Automated Information Service (BLAISE), a computerized bibliographic service open to subscribing libraries and institutions, was launched officially in December 1977 and is now available to individual users on a fee-paying basis. BLAISE currently offers access to a dozen or so data-bases in this country (BLAISE-LINE), to DIALOG in California, and to TELESYSTEMES-QUESTEL in Paris, for bibliographical references in the humanities and social sciences.

The system operates in this way: a librarian performs the search, preferably in the presence of the enquirer; the information obtained is printed off-line in Harlow and posted to the Bloomsbury Reading Room, where it may be collected a couple of days later. Off-line prints from DIALOG normally take about a week to reach London, those from Paris slightly less. Costs depend on the complexity and comprehensiveness of the search; they are calculated on the time spent connected to the computer (currently at £1.60 per minute) plus a small charge for the off-line print. The BLAISE-LINE data-bases include the Department of Printed Books Catalogue from 1976 onwards; the Eighteenth Century Short-Title Catalogue; the Incunable Short-Title Catalogue (books and other material printed during the 15th century); UKC MARC and UK MARC 71/76 and 50/70 (British books from 1950 onwards); LCC MARC, LC MARC 71 and 68 (books acquired by the Library of Congress in Washington from 1968 onwards); the British Education Index; the Conference Proceedings Index; and AV MARC (currently available audio-visual materials). Others will be added.

DIALOG is based in California. It has an enormous number of data-bases available, both on general subjects and on the humanities; there is a bias towards American material, naturally, but it does contain some coverage of British and European works.

The Paris-based TELESYSTEMES-QUESTEL offers a large number of data-bases containing material in languages other than

French. These include Francis-H (humanities) and Francis-S (social sciences), both from 1972 onwards.

Now that the Washington Library Network software has been installed (summer 1985), the computer service offered by the British Library promises to be still further improved. The service offered by the Science Reference Library, at both the Holborn and Aldwych branches, uses quite different data-bases.

The Book Trust operates a Book Information Service which will endeavour to answer up to four queries free of charge, after which a modest research fee will be payable (calculated at £6 per hour for members, £8 per hour for non-members). The direct line for this service is 01-874 8526.

Tracing books

Often the researcher wants to trace a particular book whose exact title and author he does not know. Provided he has a vague idea of either author or title, or approximate date of publication, this is not difficult, but in other cases it may involve a lengthy search.

The earliest listing in this country is a series known as the *London Catalogue of Books*, covering the period 1700-1855. The *English Catalogue of Books*, the first volume of which covers the years 1801-36, and subsequent volumes five- or three-year periods, continues until 1968. *Whitaker's Cumulative Book List* (from 1924) used to be published quarterly, with annual and five-yearly cumulations; since 1984 it has appeared annually only. The same firm issues *British Books in Print*, *Paperbacks in Print*, *Children's Books in Print* and *Religious Books in Print* annually. Most libraries now subscribe to the microfiche edition of *British Books in Print*, which updates the listing each month. For US titles there are the annual *American Books in Print* and the cumulative volumes of the *American Book Publishing Record*. Bowker's *Subject Guide to Books in Print* is another valuable source, published annually, which lists US non-fiction titles under some 62,000 subject headings, with over 55,000 cross references.

Obtaining out-of-print books

If you wish to acquire titles that are out of print, either for your own reference collection or for work on a specific project, you should make a point of informing your local antiquarian bookseller of your special interest. He will then not only let you know when suitable books are on offer, but will also advertise through the trade for books that you require; there is no charge for this service and no obligation to buy when a quotation is forthcoming, subject to the book or books remaining unsold in the meantime; but the process may take several weeks. *The Clique Annual Directory of Booksellers specialising in antiquarian and out of print books*, which is published annually and is available outside the trade from The Clique, c/o Stoate & Bishop Printers Ltd, St James's Square, Cheltenham, Glos GL50 3PU (tel. Cheltenham (0242) 36741), and Sheppard's *Directory of Dealers in Second Hand and Antiquarian Books in the British Isles* are the best sources of information for the researcher who wishes to get in direct touch with a specialist dealer. *Driff's Guide to All the Secondhand and Antiquarian Bookshops in Britain* is an informative handbook spiced with witty anecdotes and the personal observations of the compiler, and excellent value for the dedicated bookhunter.

You may also like to use the book-finding specialists such as *Bookfinders*, who have recently moved from London to Camberley, Moor Lane, Westfield, E. Sussex TN35 4QU (tel. Hastings (0424) 754291); similar services are advertised on the back page of the *Times Literary Supplement* and other papers. All of them offer to try to locate books for customers on a country-wide basis. Obtaining out-of-print books from book-finding services abroad is not so satisfactory: by the time the quotation is received and the bank transfer effected, so often the books have been sold to another customer (but see the chapter on 'Information from Foreign Sources', page 124).

The *Books on Demand* programme marketed by University Microfilms International of White Swan House, Godstone, Surrey RH9 8LW (tel. Godstone (0883) 844123) has some 100,000 titles and 47 subject bibliographies for sale on microfilm; these are regularly updated. There is an author index (latest edition 1983).

'Books in progress'

The 'Books in Progress' scheme, operated originally by the National Book League and later by the Arts Council, and mentioned in the previous edition of this handbook, has been discontinued.

Newspapers and periodicals

The major holding in this country of national and foreign papers and periodicals is at the British Library Reference Division, Department of Printed Books: newspapers and weeklies at the British Library

Newspaper Library, Colindale Avenue, London NW9 5HE (tel. 01-200 5515), opposite Colindale Underground station; all other periodicals at the main Library in Bloomsbury, where they are normally read in the North Library Gallery. (The few exceptions to this division are that all London newspapers published before 1801, as well as the *London, Edinburgh, Belfast* and *Dublin Gazettes* and all newspapers published in oriental languages are kept at Bloomsbury, where there are also duplicate runs of *The Times* (on microfilm), *The Times Literary Supplement* and the *Illustrated London News* (1844-1892); these are applied for in the usual way in the main Reading Room. A British Library ticket also admits to Colindale, and short-term tickets will be issued on application in person to the Superintendent in the search room.

There is a card-index catalogue at the Newspaper Library (with a duplicate at Bloomsbury) listing alphabetically by title all the papers held, with dates. The researcher using this index should remember that where there are several papers or magazines of the same title, the cards are arranged within the title alphabetically under the place of publication.

The British Library Newspaper Library is currently in the process of an extensive programme of microfilming, with a view to relieving pressure on the handling of the original newsprint; for some years now most current foreign papers have been purchased only on microfilm. This is a great convenience both to the reader and to the library staff, since in many cases up to a year's run of a paper or journal can be housed on one spool, thus eliminating the handling of bulky volumes and conserving storage space. Microfilms of newspapers and journals are currently on sale at £24 per reel (£12 per half-reel). Photographic or electrostatic enlargements may be obtained from microfilm, and photocopies (a whole page or double spread, according to size, slightly reduced) may be ordered at 50p a sheet plus VAT, subject to the usual copyright regulations (only one article from any one issue of a paper or periodical at any one time). Where photocopies are ordered by post, there is a minimum charge and the Library also levies a handling charge.

Tracing newspapers and periodicals

The researcher wishing to trace an early English language newspaper will find all those published in Great Britain and Ireland in the period 1801-1900 listed in the *British Museum Catalogue of Printed Books Supplement: Newspapers*; the arrangement is by place of publication, but there is a title index. Papers published prior to 1800 are included in the *British Museum Catalogue of Printed Books: Periodical Publications*. Both these printed BM catalogues are usually available at major reference libraries.

Another very useful source for early newspapers is G. A. Cranfield's *Handlist of English provincial newspapers and periodicals, 1700-1760. Willing's Press Guide*, first published in 1871 as *Frederick May's London Press Directory*, and now issued annually, is one of the best quick reference guides to modern newspapers and periodicals in the United Kingdom; recent editions also cover the principal publications of Europe, the United States, the Gulf States, Australasia and the Far East. A complete set of *Willing's*, and also the earlier *European Press Guide*, is on the open shelves at Colindale; it contains an A-Z list, a list of publications under subjects, and a list under English counties and towns. The *Tercentenary Handlist of English and Welsh Newspapers, Magazines and Reviews*, in two parts (I, London; II, Provincial), lists papers and journals under the date on which they were first issued (useful if you want to know what was published in a particular period); there is also a title list. Recently published is *The Newspaper Press in Britain*, an annotated bibliography edited by David Linton and Ray Boston.

So far as foreign newspapers are concerned, the *Europa Year Book* gives details of the press of each country; and volume 3 of the *Guide to Reference Material* lists the various national source books under each country in both the 'Newspapers' and 'Periodicals' sections.

Benn's Media Directory (formerly *Benn's Press Directory*) covers the whole world and is the oldest-established media guide: now in two volumes, the latest edition (1986) is 134th in a series directly descended from *Mitchell's Newspaper Press Directory*, which was first published in 1846. It covers newspapers, periodicals, house journals, and much other related information on embassies and High Commissions, news agencies, broadcasting, and all aspects of the media including, from the 1986 edition, cable and satellite. Subscribers are entitled to use a unique information service – *Benn's Media Information Service* (BEMIS) – which will answer spot queries on UK or overseas media free of charge; should any enquiry need extensive research, this is costed individually before the work is undertaken. The Directory is not cheap, and is probably beyond the pocket of individual researchers, but the local library is almost certainly a subscriber and enquiries may be channelled through them. Write or telephone to the Editor, BEMIS, Benn Business Information Services Ltd, PO Box 20, Sovereign Way, Tonbridge, Kent TN9 1RQ (tel. Tonbridge (0732) 362666).

In the general catalogue at the British Library periodicals are entered in a series of volumes filed under 'P' and headed 'Periodical

Publications'; the titles are arranged alphabetically under the place of publication. The transactions or proceedings of most learned societies are not here, but catalogued under the name of the society. It is necessary, therefore, first to look in the general catalogue under the title of the periodical, which will give either a finding reference to 'Periodical Publications' (i.e. the place of publication) or to the name of the relevant society, which may be catalogued under a particular country, town or university. This sounds more complicated than it is in practice, and you will very quickly get into the swing of it. Periodicals which are not catalogued may be at the British Library Lending Division; ask at the enquiry desk how to obtain them.

Several other major libraries publish lists of their holdings of newspapers and periodicals; until recently the best source was the *British Union-Catalogue of Periodicals*, an alphabetical listing by title, which recorded the whereabouts of all newspapers and periodicals of the world from the 17th century to the present day held in British libraries, with the dates held. There was also the *World List of Scientific Periodicals published in the years 1900-1960*, which was later incorporated into the *British Union-Catalogue: New Periodical Titles*. These have now been replaced by *Serials in the British Library*. *Ulrich's International Periodicals Directory* contains information on 70,000 periodicals published worldwide; it is updated every six weeks on the Ulrich's data-base (available 'on-line' via DIALOG). Another useful reference tool is C. E. Wall's *Periodical Title Abbreviations*. The first volume of Walford's *Guide to Current British Periodicals* was published in 1985, and this promises to be as useful to the researcher as the same compiler's *Guide to Reference Material*, referred to several times in this handbook. Cynthia L. White's *Women's Magazines 1693-1968* is a first-class survey of that field and will enable you to find out which magazines were in circulation at a particular date and what they contained. Finally, use should be made of the microfiche *Keyword Index to Serial Titles (KIST)*, which indexes some 200,000 titles (with 39,000 cross references) in the British Library Lending Division and the Science Reference Library.

Now that *The Times* is on microfilm, you should have no difficulty in finding a library in your region where you may have access to the complete run, starting with the first issue of 1 January 1785. Other papers may not be so easy to find in the provinces, but a complete list of newspapers (worldwide) that are available on film may be obtained from Research Publications Ltd, 77 Milford Road, Reading RG1 8LG (tel. Reading (0734) 583247), should you wish to purchase reels for private use.

Indexes to newspapers

The most valuable of British newspaper indexes to the researcher is the *Index to The Times*. The official index has been published since 1906, and an earlier, slightly less accurate version, known as *Palmer's Index to The Times*, from 1790 to June 1941. The *Index* is now published monthly, with annual cumulations; since 1973 it has included references to the *Sunday Times*, *Times Literary Supplement*, *Educational Supplement* and *Higher Education Supplement*. The *Index* is useful not only for verifying reports in *The Times* itself, but as a guide to the dates of reports to be found elsewhere. Other newspapers in the United Kingdom which publish or have at one time published indexes are the *Financial Times* (May 1912-1920, and more recently from 1981), the *Glasgow Herald* (annually from 1907), and *The Guardian* (from 1986). These indexes are on the open shelves at Colindale and other good reference libraries, together with indexes to several American papers such as the *New York Times, Washington Post, Chicago Tribune* and *Los Angeles Times*, and indexes to a few Commonwealth and foreign newspapers. A photocopied list of indexes available at the Newspaper Library in Colindale may be had on request in the Reading Room. Most major Libraries subscribe to the *Times Index*, not so many to the index to the *New York Times*.

Indexes to periodicals

The earliest index to periodicals is *Poole's Index to Periodical Literature*, which covers the period 1802-1906; it has a comparatively recent author index which is extremely useful. There are also the '*Review of Reviews' Index* to periodicals in the years 1890-1902 and the *Wellesley Index to Victorian Periodicals*, 1824-1900, among others. The *Reader's Guide to Periodical Literature* is an American publication that has been issued since 1900; its English equivalent, the *Subject Index to Periodicals*, first published in 1915, changed its name in 1962 to the *British Humanities Index*, and is now published quarterly, with annual cumulations. Other more specialised periodicals indexes include the *Current Technology Index* (which has replaced the *British Technology Index*), the *British Education Index*, and a series published by H. W. Wilson of New York, of which the *Art Index*, the *Biography Index*, the *Humanities Index* and the *Social Sciences Index* (the last two formerly published as one index 1965-74, and before that date as the *International Index*), are the most likely to be of interest to the UK writer/researcher.

Among the indexes to particular magazines which are of immense value to researchers are those to the *Gentleman's Magazine*: the printed index volumes cover the period 1731-1819, with separate indexes to the biographical and obituary notices. *Notes and Queries* carries indexes to each volume and cumulated indexes for every twelve volumes. Both of these publications are excellent sources of information on a variety of subjects. Among recent indexing projects has been the index compiled by Geraldine Beare to the *Strand Magazine 1891-1950*, also of great value.

The majority of modern periodicals carry volume indexes, and these are a great help in tracing material quickly. Where there are no such printed indexes, it is necessary to skim through the contents page of each issue to find a particular paper or feature, or the researcher can apply to the editorial office of the publication concerned, if this is still in existence, where a card index may be held.

Most public libraries keep long runs of local newspapers, county magazines and publications of their local historical and archaeological societies; these will also be found on the shelves of county record offices.

The British Library Science Reference Library, whose collection is split between the Holborn and Aldwych branches, houses a vast number of scientific and technical periodicals, including those formerly at the Patent Office Library.

The researcher wishing to trace a medical paper should do so in the *Index Medicus*, to which most medical libraries subscribe; this index covers some 2,300 periodicals worldwide.

Press cuttings

Mention of press cuttings was absent from previous editions of this handbook, and I have been taken to task for the omission. The reason for it was a personal one, since in my experience artificial collections of this nature are not to be regarded as reliable source-material: they are as reliable and comprehensive only insofar as the person assembling the cuttings was reliable and conscientious. However, they do have a value – as a starting-point in research – and should not have been dismissed out of hand. The best advice to be given here is: use them, but use with care, and never as a substitute for original research.

Many newspapers, libraries, trade and professional bodies maintain cuttings collections, and it is always worth asking what they have and having a look at them: you may well pick up leads for further research in this way.

Official Publications

Research in the field of government and official publications is complex and beyond the scope of this handbook. Two excellent modern guides are Frank Rodgers' *Guide to British Government Publications* and Stephen Richards' *Directory of British Official Publications*. Her Majesty's Stationery Office issues *Sectional Lists* which carry details of departmental publications; these are revised regularly and are available free of charge from HMSO and from booksellers who are HMSO agents. The most useful of these to the researcher is Sectional List No. 24, *British National Archives*. Another free leaflet of interest is *Government Statistics: a brief guide to sources*, produced by the Central Statistical Office and published by HMSO. Publications of some 400 British official organizations are listed in the *Catalogue of British Official Publications Not Published by HMSO*.

Most British official publications are available at the main reference libraries and public libraries. The British Library Reference Division Official Publications Collection (formerly known as the State Paper Room), in the King Edward Building of the British Museum, houses government publications of all countries, publications of the United Nations and other international and inter-governmental bodies. British Parliamentary papers, complete sets of *Hansard* and the *London Gazette*, current UK electoral registers and all the main statistical yearbooks are among a large number of reference books on the open shelves. The library is open at the same times as the main British Library Reading Room, and delivery of books tends to be rather more prompt. However, certain publications are out-housed at Woolwich, so that you should be prepared for a delay of up to 48 hours in this case.

Researchers seeking information on the United Nations and its specialized agencies may use the library of the United Nations Information Centre, Ship House, 20 Buckingham Gate, London SW1 (tel. 01-630 1981).

Miscellaneous

The *Essay and General Literature Index*, covering work published since 1900, is the best place to look for miscellaneous articles, reviews, etc.; now issued twice a year, with monthly previews and regularly cumulated volumes, it is normally available in the larger reference libraries.

To check quotations it is best to look first in the 'standard' works

– *The Oxford Dictionary of Quotations, Bartlett's Familiar Quotations* and *Benham's Book of Quotations, Proverbs and Household Words*. There are many other collections, and some more modern compilations are mentioned later in this handbook, in Appendix II 'Reference Books for the Writer', pages 177-8. Use should also be made of concordances to the Bible, to Shakespeare, Tennyson and many other major writers; people tend to forget just how time-saving these can be when one is reasonably sure of the author and when one has a major word or phrase to go on. *Granger's Index to Poetry*, with its title, first line, author and subject indexes, is of course indispensable. The *Song Index* and its supplement are useful sources for songs up to 1934, and there is also the *Song Catalogue* section of the *BBC Music Library Catalogue of Holdings*; the *Popular Song Index* and its supplements bring the catalogues up to the present time. For music bibliographies and catalogues of printed music – outside the scope of this handbook – see volume 3 of the *Guide to Reference Material*, under 'Music', and the Music Catalogue in the British Library.

If you need to check on any particular kind of literature or printed matter – for example, hymns or nursery rhymes – you should always look in the subject index of the reference library first, to find out the standard work.

Translations

The best source is the *Index Translationum*, which has been published since 1932; it is now issued annually by UNESCO, and most reference libraries subscribe to it.

Street and telephone directories

The Guildhall Library in London has a collection of street directories from the late 18th century, and so has the Westminster History Collection of Westminster City Libraries, at 158-160 Buckingham Palace Road, London SW1W 9UD. Most county record offices have sets of their local directories. These are extremely useful for checking addresses and names of neighbours, in biographical and family history research, as are the court guides (for the aristocracy) which also date from the late 18th century. The yellow pages of modern telephone directories will help you if you want to contact experts in a particular field.

Maps

There is a Map Library at the British Museum, which is open to students, and the Public Record Office, most local record offices and some libraries, such as Birmingham Central Reference Library, have special historical collections. The *Catalogue of Printed Maps in the British Museum* and volume 3 of the *Catalogue of the National Maritime Museum Library* are good source-guides.

Stanford's International Map Centre, 12-14 Long Acre, London WC2E 2LP (tel. 01-836 1321) sells antique and modern maps and atlases covering the world. The first edition of the Ordnance Survey has been reprinted, and the historical series is still available; the modern editions, in various scales, may be purchased from HMSO or their main agents, the London Map Centre, 22-24 Caxton Street, London SW1H 0QU (tel. 01-222 2466), or ordered from most booksellers. J. B. Harley's *Ordnance Survey Maps: A Descriptive Manual* is a useful handbook; while forthcoming soon from the Royal Historical Society will be a *Guide to Maps*.

Unpublished Sources

Manuscripts and Private Papers

The major source of manuscripts in England is the Department of Manuscripts at the British Museum, part of the British Library Reference Division. The British Library's reader's ticket does not admit researchers to the Students' Room of the Department of MSS – a separate ticket must be applied for at the entrance to the Department. Details of the holdings will be found in T. C. Skeat's *The Catalogues of the Manuscript Collections in the British Museum*, while for quick reference there is M. A. E. Nickson's more recent booklet, *The British Library: Guide to the Catalogues and Indexes of the Department of Manuscripts*, which also lists the reference books available in the Students' Room and the locations there of catalogues of MSS held in other libraries. The Chadwyck-Healey *Index of Manuscripts in the British Library* contains entries for over a million persons and places in collections acquired by the Department of MSS up to 1950. Recent acquisitions, catalogued as Add. MSS, are by number in a series of volumes on the open shelves in the Students' Room.

If you wish to trace the location of other manuscripts or ascertain whether any private papers exist, or to find out if such papers have been deposited or registered, you should first get in touch with the Royal Commission on Historical Manuscripts, Quality House, Quality Court, Chancery Lane, London WC2A 1HP. The Commission maintains a National Register of Archives, consisting of some 28,000 unpublished reports on privately owned records and those held in repositories other than the Public Record Office. The HMSO *Sectional List* No. 17 is devoted to publications of the Commission, which include over 200 volumes of reports and a most useful *Guide to Sources for British History* series, of which four volumes have been published to date: 1 *Papers of British Cabinet Ministers 1782-1900*; 2 *The Manuscript Papers of British Scientists 1600-1940*; 3 *Guide to the Location of Collections described in the Reports and Calendars Series 1870-1980*; and 4 *Private Papers of British Diplomats 1782-1900*.

The search room of the Commission is open to the public, and enquiries may be made in person or in writing (addressed to the Registrar), but not by telephone.

An excellent finding aid to unpublished material is the Chadwyck-Healey *National Inventory of Documentary Sources in the United Kingdom*, on microfiche, updated eight times a year. Most major libraries subscribe, and there are useful leaflets explaining how to use the Inventory. *British Archives: A Guide to Archive Resources in the United Kingdom*, by Janet Foster and Julia Sheppard, is another indispensable reference tool, listing some 700 archive collections by town, by county and alphabetically; the introduction contains useful advice to the first-time user of archival material.

Public records

The Public Record Office holds archives going back to the 11th century; nowadays all official records are automatically deposited within thirty years and (with certain exceptions) are open to the public thirty years after their creation. The bulk of the records were moved in 1976 from the old building in Chancery Lane to a modern one in Kew, but a few classes of records have been retained in central London; a list of these is available from the PRO, or intending researchers may write or telephone for information, either to Ruskin Avenue, Kew, Richmond, Surrey TW9 4DU (tel. 01-876 3444) or to Chancery Lane, London WC2A 1LR (tel. 01-405 0741). Readers' tickets (valid for several years) or temporary tickets for short periods are obtainable at both places.

At the PRO documents are ordered by computer, and readers are issued with bleepers which let them know when they can collect from the issue desk. Qualified staff are on hand to deal with enquiries and to explain how to operate the computer terminals. There is a large typing room, as well as good facilities for ordering photocopies and microfilms. Documents are classified by Department or Ministry rather than by subject, so that it is necessary to know first of all (or to find out) to which class the documents you need belong. You then look up the class lists of the relevant date, in order to find the piece numbers (files) you have to order. It is not as complicated as it sounds, and the PRO issues a number of excellent information leaflets on various subjects which are of much help to the novice.

Parliamentary records from 1497 are at the House of Lords Record Office, and records of British rule in India to 1947 at the India Office Records Offce, 197 Blackfriars Road, London SE1 8NG. The Imperial War Museum, Lambeth Road, London SE1 6HZ, houses documentary and illustrative material on the two World Wars, and Churchill College Archives Centre, Cambridge CB3 0DS, is collecting papers of 20th-century politicians, scientists, military and naval commanders, but not all of these are yet open to the public.

At the Guildhall Library in London you will find records relating to the City from medieval times, including those of many of the City livery companies (although some of these perished in the Great Fire of 1666).

The National Library of Scotland possesses a priceless collection of manuscripts, ranging from early monastic writings to modern political papers; there are printed and manuscript indexes. There is also the National Register of Archives (Scotland), a branch of the Scottish Record Office, General Register House, Edinburgh EH1 3YY. M. Livingstone's *Guide to the Public Records of Scotland*, although published as long ago as 1905, is still a useful work of reference, and the 2-volume *List of Gifts and Deposits in the Scottish Record Office* describes briefly the family muniments and business records that make up this collection.

If you seek Irish records, contact the Public Record Office of Northern Ireland, 66 Balmoral Avenue, Belfast BT9 6NY. The old Public Record Office in Dublin was destroyed in 1922, but the National Library of Ireland, Kildare Street, Dublin, and Trinity College Library in the same city both possess fine collections of historical manuscripts.

HMSO *Sectional List* No. 24, *British National Archives*, lists the publications of the Public Record Office, the Public Record Office of Northern Ireland, the Scottish Record Office and the House of Lords Record Office. Some of the older record publications have been reprinted by the Kraus-Thomson Organization Ltd, which has also microfilmed some classes of unpublished records; reprints and microfilms may be purchased through HMSO.

Theses

It is always worthwhile checking on dissertations, as these can be a most valuable source of information. Aslib has since 1950 published an *Index to Theses accepted for Higher Degrees in the Universities of Great Britain and Ireland*, and the universities of Oxford, Cambridge and London publish separate annual lists. There are *Abstracts of Dissertations* for Oxford and Cambridge going back to 1925, and lists for London in the University Calendar 1930-40, as well as *Subjects of Dissertations, Theses etc. for Higher Degrees* covering 1937-51.

For American theses, the *Comprehensive Dissertation Index 1861-1972* is the best source; supplementary volumes are issued annually. A wide range of dissertations submitted to North American universities may be obtained on microfilm from University Microfilms International, White Swan House, Godstone, Surrey RH9 8LW; catalogues on a variety of subjects are available on request.

Indexes to foreign theses are printed in *Guide to Reference Material*, volume 3, under 'Theses'. See also a most useful handbook, D. H. Borchardt and J. D. Thawley's *Guide to Availability of Theses*.

Filmed and recorded material

The researcher interested in filmed material and the history of the cinema should contact the National Film Archive, 81 Dean Street, London W1V 6AA (tel. 01-437 4355). The Archive publishes a comprehensive catalogue relating to films of all countries.

The British Library National Sound Archive (formerly the British Institute of Recorded Sound), 29 Exhibition Road, London SW7 2AS (tel. 01-589 6603) has been collecting material for the past 35 years; it now holds almost a million disks of various kinds and some 35,000 hours of recorded tape. A free listening service is available to the public, by appointment, and transcripts (on tape) will be supplied, subject to proper copyright clearance. The Archive's information service will assist researchers in the location of particular recordings, and the library is open to the public without formality. It is hoped eventually to publish a National Register of Collections of Recorded Sound; in the meanwhile the information is maintained at the National Sound Archive in machine-readable form (i.e. on disk).

Broadcast and televised material

The BBC Data Service, established in 1981, offers a fast and efficient research service on a subscription or fee-paying basis (currently £35 per hour for occasional use), drawing on the unique store of information gathered internationally by the British Broadcasting Corporation over the years. Enquiries should be addressed to: BBC Data Enquiry Service, Room 3, The Langham, BBC, Portland Place, London W1A 1AA (tel. 01-927 5998).

Use may also be made of the BBC Written Archives Centre, Caversham Park, Reading RG4 8TZ (tel. Reading (0734) 472742. The Centre is open to students and *bona fide* researchers, or staff will undertake research at an hourly rate. The BBC Sound Archives are not open to the public, but it is sometimes possible to obtain information by letter and, occasionally, by special permission, to listen to recordings. Addresses and telephone numbers of the BBC and of the Independent Broadcasting Authority and all local radio stations are given in the current *Writers' & Artists' Yearbook*.

Most good reference libraries possess the three BBC catalogues on microfiches produced by Chadwyck-Healey Ltd of Cambridge: *BBC Radio: Author and Title Catalogues of Transmitted Drama, Poetry and Features 1929-1975*; *BBC Television: Author and Title Catalogues of Transmitted Drama and Features 1936-1975 (with Chronological List of Transmitted Plays)*; and the *BBC Programme Index*, annually from 1979, covering radio and television, which consists of a main index, a titles index, a subject index and a contributors' index. Once you have ascertained the date, programme title and name of the producer, you will be able to write a suitable letter in the hope of obtaining a transcript or, perhaps, permission to view or hear a recording (if this is not already at the National Sound Archive).

Two useful paperbacks that will help with all media contacts are Denis MacShane's *Using the Media* and Jane Drinkwater's *Get It on Radio and Television*; and it should not be overlooked that both the BBC and the IBA publish annual yearbooks.

Oral history collections

Although the term 'oral history' is a fairly recent one, in fact this was the very first kind of history, as Paul Thompson has pointed out in *The Voice of the Past*. The growth of oral history study groups today reflects an interest and awareness of the value of this field of research, which demands quite different skills from those of the historian who handles only documentation.

Researchers interested in the subject would do well to subscribe to *Oral History*, the journal of the Oral History Society. The Society's *Directory of British Oral Collections* (volume 1 only) is an alphabetical listing, with subject and place indexes, while the more comprehensive American publication, *Oral History Collections*, lists both US and foreign collections, by state and by country respectively.

It is a sobering thought that by the year 2000 only some 50% of all records may be on paper, as opposed to film, tape and computer storage systems. Future researchers will therefore spend an increasingly greater proportion of their working time looking and listening instead of poring over the printed or handwritten page in library and record office, and no doubt there will soon be many more facilities of this nature. Like it or not, the revolution is under way, and we are going to have to get used to it, so the sensible thing to do is to prepare ourselves by acquiring the necessary new skills.

Abstracts of Dissertations approved for the PhD, MSc and MLitt Degrees 1925/6-1956/7, Cambridge University Press, 1927-59

Abstracts of Dissertations for the Degree of Doctor of Philosophy 1925-40, Oxford University Press, 12 vols, 1928-47 (BLitt and BSc theses are included in vols 10 and 12)

American Book Publishing Record, annual and 5-year cumulative volumes, Bowker, New York. There is a set of 15 cumulative volumes covering the years 1950-77 and an earlier cumulative volume covering 1876-1949.

Annual Directory of Booksellers specialising in Antiquarian and Out of Print Books, published by The Clique, Cheltenham

Art Index, published quarterly since 1929 by H. W. Wilson, New York

Aslib Directory of Information Sources in the United Kingdom, 2 vols, regularly brought up to date. Latest editions: 1 *Science, Technology and Commerce*, 1982; 2 *Social Sciences, Medicine and the Humanities*, 1984. Aslib, London (available for sale to non-members)

Bartlett's Familiar Quotations, 16th ed., rev., Macmillan, London, 1985

BBC Yearbook, published annually by the British Broadcasting Corporation

Benham's Book of Quotations, Proverbs and Household Words, rev. ed. with supplement, Harrap, London, 1948 (now discontinued)

Benn's Media Directory (formerly *Benn's Press Directory*), published annually by Benn Business Information Services Ltd, Tonbridge, Kent

Bibliographic Index, published since 1938 by H. W. Wilson, New York; now twice yearly, with cumulated annual and 3-year volumes

Bibliographical Services throughout the World, UNESCO, Paris, 1969

Bibliography of British Literary Bibliography, by T. H. Howard-Hill, Oxford University Press, London, 1969-, in progress

Biography Index, published since 1946 by H. W. Wilson, New York; quarterly with annual and 3-year cumulated volumes

Bookseller, The, published weekly by J. Whitaker, London

Bookshops of London, 3rd ed., by Diana Stephenson, Roger Lascelles, Brentford, 1984

Books in Print (American), published annually by R. R. Bowker, New York

British Archives: A Guide to Archive Resources in the United Kingdom, by Janet Foster and Julia Sheppard, Macmillan, London, 1982; paperback ed., 1984

British Books in Print, published annually by J. Whitaker, London; updated monthly on microfiche

British Education Index, first published in 1954; now by the British Library, Bibliographic Services Division, London; three times a year with 2-yearly cumulations

British Humanities Index, published quarterly since 1963, with annual cumulations, by the Library Association, London

British Library General Catalogue of Printed Books to 1975, Saur, London, 360 vols, 1979-86

British Library: Guide to the Catalogues and Indexes of the Department of Manuscripts, 2nd ed., by M. A. E. Nickson, British Library, London, 1982

British Museum General Catalogue of Printed Books: Periodical Publications, British Museum, London, 6 vols, 1899-1900
Supplement: Newspapers published in Great Britain and Ireland 1801-1900, British Museum, London, 1905. (For modern periodicals and newspapers see current general catalogues.)

British National Bibliography, weekly since 1950, with monthly, annual and 5-yearly cumulations; now published by the British Library, *BNB* Division, London

British Union-Catalogue of Periodicals (from 17th century to present day), Butterworth, London, 4 vols, 1955-58; *Supplement to 1960*, 1962; *New Periodical Titles*, quarterly, with annual cumulations, 1964-80.

Catalogue of British Official Publications Not Published by HMSO, published every two months, with annual cumulations, by Chadwyck-Healey Ltd, Cambridge

Catalogue of Printed Maps in the British Museum, first published 1884, now annually, British Museum, London

Catalogue of the National Maritime Museum Library, vol 3: *Atlases and Cartography*, HMSO, London, 2 vols, 1971

Catalogues of the Manuscript Collections, The, rev. ed., by T. C. Skeat, British Museum, London, 1962

Children's Books in Print, published annually since 1969 by J. Whitaker, London

Comprehensive Dissertation Index 1861-1972, University Microfilms International, Ann Arbor, Michigan, USA, annually from 1973, with 10-year cumulation volume covering 1973-82 (marketed in UK by University Microfilms International, White Swan House, Godstone, Surrey RH9 8LW)

Current Technology Index (formerly the *British Technology Index*), Library Association, London, monthly (hard copy, microfilm or tape)

Directory of British Official Publications: A Guide to Sources, by Stephen Richards, Mansell, London, 1981

Directory of British Oral Collections, by Anne McNulty and Hilary Troop, Oral History Society, Colchester, vol I, 1981

Directory of Dealers in Second-Hand and Antiquarian Books in the British Isles, Sheppard Press, London. Published every three years; latest ed. (11th), 1984-86

Directory of Specialist Bookdealers in the United Kingdom, 3rd ed., by Peter Marcan, High Wycombe, 1984

Driff's Guide to All the Secondhand & Antiquarian Bookshops in Britain, 2nd ed., BCM Driffield, London, 1985; obtainable from Holborn Books, 14 Charing Cross Road, London WC2H 0HR (tel. 01-240 2337)

English Catalogue of Books, The, first volume covering 1801-36, and subsequent volumes 3- or 5-year cumulations; now discontinued (last volume published 1969)

Essay and General Literature Index, first volume covering work published 1900-33, 1934; now half-yearly with 5-year cumulations, H. W. Wilson, New York

Europa Year Book, Europa Publications, London, 2 vols, annually

Gentleman's Magazine: General Index to the first 56 volumes (1731-86), 2 vols; *General Index ... 1787-1819, Index to the Biographical and Obituary Notices, 1731-1780* and *1781-1819*, 2 vols, 1st vol, British Record Society, London; 2nd vol, Garland, New York and London

Get It On Radio and Television, by Jane Drinkwater, Pluto, London, 1984

Glasgow Herald Index, published annually since 1907 by Outram, Glasgow

Government Statistics: A Brief Guide to Sources, Central Statistical Office, published by HMSO annually, London

Granger's Guide to Poetry, 5th ed., (first published 1904) Columbia University Press, New York, 1962; *Supplement*, 1967

Guide to Availability of Theses, by D. H. Borchardt and J. D. Thawley, Saur, Munich, 1981

Guide to British Government Publications, A, by Frank Rodgers, H. W. Wilson, New York, 1980

Guide to Current British Periodicals, ed. J. Walford and J. M. Harvey, vol 1 *Humanities and Social Sciences*, Library Association, London, 1985

Guide to Maps, Royal Historical Society, London, forthcoming

Guide to Reference Books, 9th ed., ed. Eugene P. Sheehy, American Library Association, Chicago, 1976; supplements, 1980, 1982, 1984

Guide to Reference Material, 4th edition: ed. A. J. Walford, vol 1 *Science and Technology*, 1980; vol 2 *Social and Historical Sciences, Philosophy and Religion*, 1982; vol 3 *Generalities, Languages, The Arts and Literature*, 1985; *Concise Guide to Reference Material*, 1981, Library Association, London

Guide to the Contents of the Public Record Office, HMSO, London, 3 vols, 1963-9

Guide to the Public Records of Scotland, by M. Livingstone, HMSO, London, 1905

Guide to the Records of Parliament, by M. F. Bond, HMSO, London, 1971

Handbook to County Bibliography: A Bibliography of Bibliographies relating to the Counties and Towns of Great Britain and Ireland, by A. L. Humphreys, originally published 1917; reprinted Dawson, London, 1974

Handlist of English Provincial Newspapers and Periodicals, 1700-1760, by G. A. Cranfield, Cambridge University Press, Cambridge, 1961

Humanities Index, published since 1983 by H. W. Wilson, New York; quarterly with annual cumulations

Index Medicus, published monthly since 1960, by National Library of Medicine, Washington, USA

Index of Manuscripts in the British Library, Chadwyck-Healey, Cambridge, 11 vols, 1985

Index to the Financial Times (May 1912-1920), and from 1981

published by Financial Times Business Information, London

Index to the Strand Magazine 1891-1950, by G. Beare, Greenwood, Westport, Conn. and London, 1982

Index to Theses accepted for Higher Degrees in the Universities of Great Britain and Ireland, published annually since 1950/51, Aslib, London

Index Translationum, published quarterly 1932-40 and since 1949 annually by UNESCO, Paris

International Books in Print, latest ed., 1985 1 *Author Title List*, 2 vols; 2 *Subject Guide*, 2 vols, Bowker, New York

Keyword Index to Serial Titles (KIST), British Library, London (microfiche)

Libraries in the United Kingdom and the Republic of Ireland, published annually by the Library Association, London

Libraries, Museums and Art Galleries Year Book, published every two years by Clarke, Cambridge

Library and Information Networks in the United Kingdom, by J. Burkett, Aslib, London, 1979

Library and Information Networks in W. Europe, by J. Burkett, Aslib, London, 1983

Library Resources series, published by the Library Association Reference Special and Information Section, and brought up to date regularly. Volumes issued to date: *London and SE England*; *East Anglia*; *East Midlands*; *Yorkshire and Humberside*; *Wales*; *Greater Manchester*; *SW England*; *The North-East*; *West Midlands*; *NW England*; *Channel Islands*

List of Gifts and Deposits in the Scottish Record Office, HMSO, London, 1971

London Bibliography of the Social Sciences, published since 1931, first by the London School of Economics, now for the British Library of Political and Economic Science by Mansell, London

London Catalogue of Books, series of overlapping catalogues covering the years 1700-1855 (first volume published by Bent, 1773)

National Inventory of Documentary Sources in the United Kingdom, Chadwyck-Healey, Cambridge, on microfiche, updated 8 times a year

New Cambridge Bibliography of English Literature, ed. G. Watson, I. R. Willison and J. D. Pickles, Cambridge University Press, Cambridge, 5 vols, 1969-77

Newspaper Press in Britain, The: An Annotated Bibliography, ed. D. Linton and R. Boston, Mansell, London, 1987

New York Times Index, published from 1913; semi-monthly since 1948, with annual cumulations, New York

Notes & Queries, published since 1849 by Oxford University Press, London; now six times a year, volume indexes and cumulated indexes per 12 volumes

Oral History, journal of the Oral History Society, Department of Sociology, University of Essex, Wivenhoe Park, Colchester CO4 3SQ

Oral History Collections, by A. M. Meckler and Ruth McMullin, Bowker, New York, 1975

Ordnance Survey Maps: A Descriptive Manual, by J. B. Harley, HMSO, London, 1975

Oxford Dictionary of Quotations, The, 3rd ed., Oxford University Press, London, 1980

Paperbacks in Print, published annually by J. Whitaker, London

Periodical Title Abbreviations, by C. E. Wall, Gale Research, Detroit, 1969

Poole's Index to Periodical Literature, 1802-1906, Boston, Mass., reprinted 1938 and 1969; *Cumulative Author Index*, Pierian Press, Ann Arbor, Michigan, 1971

Popular Song Index, by Patricia P. Havlice, Scarecrow Press, Metuchen, N.J., 1975; supplements, 1978, 1984

Printed Reference Material, 2nd ed., ed. Gavin L. Higgens, Library Association, London, 1984

Reader's Guide to Periodical Literature, published since 1900 by H. W. Wilson, New York, 18 times a year (includes quarterly cumulations) and annual cumulation

Religious Books in Print, published annually since 1984 by J. Whitaker, London

'*Review of Reviews' Index to Periodicals 1890-1902*, London, 13 vols, 1891-1903

Sectional Lists (Government Publications), HMSO, London, updated regularly, gratis; No. 17, *Publications of the Royal Commission on Historical Manuscripts*; No. 24, *British National Archives*

Serials in the British Library, quarterly, with annual cumulations (microfiche) since 1981

Social Sciences Index, published quarterly with annual cumulations by H. W. Wilson, New York

Song Catalogue, BBC Music Library, London, 4 vols, 1966

Song Index, by M. E. Sears and P. Crawford, H. W. Wilson, New York, 1926; *Supplement*, 1934

Subject Collections in European Libraries, 2nd ed., compiled by R. C. Lewanski, Bowker, New York and London, 1978

Subject Guide to Books in Print, published annually since 1957 by Bowker, New York and London

Subject Index to Periodicals, published annually 1915-53, then quarterly, with annual cumulations, 1954-61; now the *British Humanities Index*, *q.v.*

Subjects of Dissertations, Theses and Published Work presented by Successful Candidates at Examinations for Higher Degrees, covering 1937-51, University of London Library, London

Tercentenary Handlist of English and Welsh Newspapers, Magazines and Reviews, The Times, London, 1920

The Times Index: official index published from 1906, monthly since 1977, with annual cumulations, Reading Research Publications; also *Palmer's Index to The Times, 1790-June 1941*; work in progress on indexing back to 1785

Ulrich's International Periodicals Directory, 23rd ed., Bowker, New York, 2 vols, 1984

Using the Media, by Denis McShane, Pluto, London, 1979

Voice of the Past, The, by Paul Thompson, Oxford University Press, 1978

Wellesley Index to Victorian Periodicals, 1824-1900, ed. W. E. Houghton, University of Toronto Press and Routledge, London, 3 vols, 1966-79

Whitaker's Cumulative Book List, published since 1924 by J. Whitaker, London; annually since 1984

Willing's Press Guide, published annually by Thomas Skinner Directories, East Grinstead, W. Sussex

Women's Magazines 1693-1968, by Cynthia L. White, Michael Joseph, London, 1970

World Bibliographical Series, ed. Robert L. Collison, Clio Press, Oxford, 1977-, in progress

World Bibliography of Bibliographies, 4th ed., by T. Besterman, Lausanne, 4 vols and index, 1965-6; *Supplement 1964-1974* (from Library of Congress sources), ed. A. F. Toomey, Bowker, New York, 2 vols, 1977

World Guide to Libraries, 6th ed., by Helga Lengenfelder, Saur, Munich, 1983

World Guide to Special Libraries, by Helga Lengenfelder, Saur, Munich, 1983

World List of Scientific Periodicals 1900-1960, 4th ed., Butterworth, London, 3 vols, 1963-5; now incorporated in the *British Union-Catalogue New Periodical Titles*, *q.v.*

World of Learning, The, published biennially by Europa Publications, London, 2 vols

Writers' & Artists' Yearbook, published annually by A & C Black, London

Note. Saur publications are sold in the UK by Library Association Publishing. Bowker Publications are distributed in the UK by Butterworth; Sheppard Press books by Europa Publications.

4

Factual and Historical Research

The more research you undertake, the more you learn about sources. If you keep a careful note of every reliable source used (a card index filed under subjects is the best for easy reference), you can build up for yourself not only a unique and valuable research tool, but one that will save you hours of searching whenever a similar problem crops up in your work. It will prove its worth time and time again.

Since it is impossible in one short chapter to deal exhaustively with particular sources, some starting points only are suggested here under the two headings, 'Factual' and 'Historical' research, together with a warning of some of the pitfalls that lie in the path of the unwary. In all research you have to begin by consulting first one authoritative source, which leads you to the next, and that in turn to another, and so on, until you have satisfied yourself that you have found out all that you need to know. Patience and persistence are the essential qualities. Remember, too, that a negative result in research may have value.

Factual Research

The major difficulty here is that topical facts and figures are frequently out of date by the time they are published. The same applies to all writing on modern society, for the world is continually changing, developing faster with every day that passes. The best way round this problem is to rely on the latest printed information or data otherwise obtained at the time of submitting your typescript, but to indicate to your editor or publisher that you intend (or expect) to up-date specific points, either in the text or by means of an explanatory note, at proof stage. Then just before finally going to press you can telephone to the organization from which the original information came and ask for the most recent facts and figures available. All such up-datings must be kept to the absolute minimum, as author's corrections on proofs are very costly.

Another problem is that the bases used for the calculation of statistics vary from one subject to another, and from one organiz-ation to another, so that comparison can be, at worst, highly dangerous, and at best, misleading; often, also, you may find it impossible to obtain the precise breakdown you seek. Without expert help and knowledge it is unwise to meddle with statistics: where these do not exactly fit the context, the best solution is to quote them as they are presented and to add a footnote to this effect.

Sources of factual information

Mention has been made in earlier chapters of the computer search services that have recently become available. Although their use will undoubtedly become more widespread within the next few years, it is unlikely that they will be within the reach of all freelance writers for some time to come. Therefore most factual research will continue, for the time being, to be drawn from printed sources and from personal contact with authoritative experts in the field or with press and public relations officers.

Encyclopedias provide an excellent starting point, but they should always be supplemented by reference to the latest yearbooks. In order to find out what yearbooks exist on a given subject, you should consult the international directory, *Irregular Serials and Annuals*; this has a title and a subject index. Among general publications most useful to the English writer for quick reference are *Whitaker's Almanack*, *The Statesman's Year Book*, *Britain: An Official Hand-book*, *The Annual Register of World Events*, and the *Europa Year Book* (which, in spite of its title, now covers the whole world).

The Times newspaper is the best source for recent events; its *Index* is now published monthly, with annual cumulations. *Keesing's Contemporary Archives* of world events began in July 1931 as a weekly diary; cumulative indexes are now incorporated twice a year, and annually; it has a good reputation, and most reference libraries subscribe to it.

So far as UK statistics are concerned, among the best handbooks are the Central Statistical Office's *Guide to Official Statistics* and F. G. Lock's *General Sources of Statistics* (volume 5 of the *Reviews of UK Statistical Sources* series, sponsored by the Royal Statistical Society and the Social Science Research Council). The Central Statistical Office also publishes a *Monthly Digest* and an *Annual Abstract of Statistics*.

On facts in general, a handy paperback containing information in various fields for the decade 1960-1970 is *Facts in Focus*. The *Guinness Book of Records* is another surprisingly useful source-book. There are many more.

How to trace books and how to use bibliographies, concordances and books of quotations have been discussed in the previous chapter. There have been some useful general guides to factual research, as recommended in earlier editions of this handbook, but they are all now out of print. The latest to go out of print was G. Chandler's *How to Find Out: Printed and On-Line Sources*; snap it up if you see it in a secondhand bookshop.

The staff of the *Daily Telegraph* Information Bureau (tel. 01-353 4242) will answer telephoned queries from journalists and members of the public on factual, non-specialist subjects or matters that have been reported in that newspaper; they cannot, however, undertake extensive research, although they can – and frequently do – suggest where the enquirer should go for further information. For the researcher in need of a quick, straightforward answer to a factual query this is a most valuable service – and it costs only the telephone call!

Getting hold of experts

You may often find yourself at a loss as to how to get in touch with experts on particular subjects when there is no one in your immediate circle who can help. Here the best advice to be given is, 'Do not be shy. Go straight to the horse's mouth' – in other words, look up the professional or trade association concerned (or it may be an international company, a bank, or almost any other kind of group), and either write or telephone to the general secretary, press or public relations officer. Remember that all these people have a vested interest in being portrayed correctly, and also that the expert is always flattered to be consulted. If the person you approach is too busy or unable for some other reason to give you what you want, he will usually be able to suggest an alternative contact.

The best way to find out if there is a relevant association is to look in the current *Directory of British Associations and Associations in Ireland* or *Trade Associations and Professional Bodies of the United Kingdom*. Another goldmine of information of this nature, and fully up-to-date, is the *Hollis Press & Public Relations Annual*, which lists an enormous number of press contacts (with addresses and telephone numbers) in virtually every field of professional, industrial and commercial life, as well as official and public information sources, PR consultancies and much other invaluable data. There is also a list of societies and institutions in *Whitaker's Almanack*, but this is not so informative, nor is it as comprehensive as the two publications mentioned above. Lastly, do not overlook the yellow pages of telephone directories, in case there is some contact on your own doorstep.

The *NUJ Freelance Directory*, in its latest edition, is a computerised catalogue of over 1,000 freelance journalists in Britain and Ireland (and some overseas), listed alphabetically, geographically and by subject speciality. It is available at modest cost to those who are not members of the National Union of Journalists and has a useful rôle to play in the finding of local contacts.

Historical Research

Recommended studies of English historical sources are J. J. Bagley's *Historical Interpretations*, covering the period from 1066 to the present day, and the comprehensive *English Historical Documents* series, from *c.* 500 to 1914. *Sources in British Political History 1900-1951* is a good guide to 20th century historical archives, while *British Political Facts 1900-1985* is invaluable for quick reference. The HMSO *Sectional List* No. 24, *British National Archives*, lists all the published official records, including reprints.

For the researcher who wishes to delve more deeply there are some excellent bibliographies: the *Bibliography of British History* series consists of separate volumes for each period from the earliest times to 1914, while the rather more selective, but no less useful, *Bibliographical Handbooks* published by Cambridge University Press for the Conference on British Studies cover the period 1066-1970. G. R. Elton's *Modern Historians on British History 1485-1945* is a useful evaluation of recent studies.

As far as general histories are concerned, *The Cambridge Ancient History, The Cambridge Medieval History* and *The New Cambridge Modern History* are standard works. The American Historical Association's *Guide to Historical Literature*, sub-divided into countries and subjects, is an extremely valuable reference tool which is international in scope. William W. Langer's *An Encyclopedia of World History* is a superb one-volume work of reference, chronologically arranged from prehistory to the modern period.

The Oxford History of England is the authoritative work on English history, while a reliable and inexpensive paperback series handy to keep at your elbow while working is the 9-volume *Pelican History of England*; also useful are G. M. Trevelyan's *History of England* (in one volume) and Winston S. Churchill's *History of the English-Speaking Peoples*. An entirely new publication, *The Cambridge Historical Encyclopedia of Great Britain and Ireland*, with contributions from 60 major historians in a single volume, is proving to be an essential reference tool for all historical researchers: it consists of seven chronological sections, each followed by interpretative articles written by specialists, with useful marginal notes and cross-references, plus a biographical Who's Who and an index. At the other end of the scale, as a quick reminder of the dates of kings and queens, and the salient points of each reign, you cannot better Ronald Hamilton's *Now I Remember*. HMSO *Sectional List* No. 60 lists the official *Histories of the First and Second World Wars*; see also, for this period, the PRO handbook, *The Second World War: A Guide to Documents in the Public Record Office*.

Space does not permit the inclusion here of historical sources of other countries, but the reader is referred to chapter 9, 'Information from Foreign Sources' (pages 124-40) and also to volume 3 of the *Guide to Reference Material*, under 'Ancient History', 'Medieval and Modern History' and under the appropriate area of the world (or individual countries).

Conflicting authorities

One of the main problems that you must be prepared to encounter in historical research is that of conflicting authorities. Inevitably at some stage in your work you will come across two, if not three, or more, different dates or interpretations of the same event. How do you know which one to trust?

Wherever possible, you should yourself go back to the original, contemporary source. If this is not feasible, you have the choice of either weighing up the theories advanced by the various historians and coming down firmly on one side – and sticking to it – or, if you have the space and the inclination, of giving an account of the conflicting views and your reasons for preferring one to all others.

Dates

The different reckonings of dates in historical documents often confuse the beginner. Under the Julian calendar, which was in universal use throughout the Middle Ages and in some countries, such as England and Russia, until as late as the 18th and early 20th centuries respectively, the year began on 25 March. The Gregorian calendar, in which 1 January was reckoned as the beginning of each year, was introduced on the Continent in 1582, when ten days were cut out of that year in order to take care of accumulated errors of reckoning. This new calendar was not adopted in England until 1752, although for some years prior to that date a double indication was normally given in official documents (and in some private papers) for dates falling between 1 January and 24 March, as, for example, '24 February 1655/6'. The trap is that during the period 1582-1752 a traveller could leave, say, Italy, on one date and arrive in England several days earlier, because of the discrepancy in the calendar. From the end of the 16th century most English official correspondence with foreign powers carries either both dates, i.e. '12/22 December 1635', or an indication of the reckoning used, i.e. 'O.S.' (Old Style) or 'N.S.' (New Style).

The practice followed by most modern historians is to take the beginning of the historical year as 1 January. All dates between 1 January and 24 March are thus written as, for example, '22 February 1559' rather than '22 February 1558/9', except in quoted matter, where the date should always be copied faithfully as in the original text and an explanatory 'O.S.' or 'N.S.' added in square brackets if necessary. For a full discussion of this whole question, see C. R. Cheney's *Handbook of Dates for Students of English History*. This useful book contains, among other information, tables of regnal years, Easter days and calendars for all possible dates of Easter from AD 500 to the year 2000, which will enable the researcher to avoid the most common errors of dating in historical work. Another standard reference work on the subject is the *Handbook of British Chronology*, edited by F. M. Powicke and E. B. Fryde.

Dates in private papers sometimes cause the researcher a headache. Letter-writers not infrequently give an incomplete date or omit it altogther, and another trap to watch out for is that at the new year people through the ages have tended to forget, writing, for example, '5 January 1888' when they meant '5 January 1889'. Where neither contents nor letterheading provide the answer, and the date does not become clear as research progresses, you will have to choose between doing without that particular document and hazarding an intelligent guess – in which case you should make it clear that the original is undated.

The use of periodicals in historical research

Periodicals of interest to the historical researcher include the *Bulletin of the Institute of Historical Research*, the Historical Association's *History*, and *History Today*, all of which should be checked for recent studies relevant to the job in hand. Women's magazines and newspapers are an excellent source for fashion, prices and entertainments at a particular date, and papers such as *The Tatler & Bystander* and *Illustrated London News* provide useful background information on the social scene. Advertisements sometimes yield as much information as textual material.

The Historical Association's *Guide to Historical Periodicals in the English Language*, one of a series of 'Helps for Students of History' pamphlets, is now out of print, but may still be available in your local library or record office.

Annual Abstracts of Statistics, Central Statistical Office, HMSO, London

Annual Register of World Events, now published by Longman, London

Bibliographical Handbooks series, published by Cambridge University Press for the Conference on British Studies: *Anglo-Norman England 1066-1154*, ed. M. Altschul; *The High Middle Ages in England 1154-1377*, ed. B. Wilkinson; *Late-Medieval England 1377-1485*, ed. D. J. Guth; *Tudor England 1485-1603*, ed. M. Levine; *The Seventeenth Century*, ed. D. Berkowitz; *Restoration England 1660-1689*, ed. W. L. Sachse; *Late Georgian and Regency England 1760-1837*, ed. R. A. Smith; *Victorian England 1837-1901*, ed. J. L. Altholz; *Modern England 1901-1970*, ed. A. F. Havighurst

Bibliography of British History, 6 vols to date, regularly brought up to date, published by Oxford University Press: *English History to 1485*, ed. E. B. Graves; *Tudor Period, 1485-1603*, ed. Conyers Read; *Stuart Period, 1603-1714*, ed. M. F. Keeler; *The Eighteenth Century, 1714-1789*, ed. S. Pargellis and D. J. Medley; *British History 1789-1851*, ed. L. M. Brown and I. R. Christie; *British History 1851-1914*, ed. H. J. Hanham

Britain: an Official Handbook, HMSO, London, annually

British National Archives, Government Publications *Sectional List* No. 24, HMSO, London, revised regularly

British Political Facts 1900-1979, 6th ed., by David Butler and Gareth Butler, Macmillan, London, 1985

Bulletin of the Institute of Historical Research, published twice a year since 1923

Cambridge Ancient History, The, 12 vols of text, 5 vols of plates (some vols now revised), first published by Cambridge University Press, 1923-39

Cambridge Historical Encyclopedia of Great Britain and Ireland, The, ed. Christopher Haigh, Cambridge University Press, 1985

Cambridge Medieval History, The, 8 vols, plus portfolios of maps (some vols now revised), first published by Cambridge University Press, 1911-36

Directory of British Associations and Associations in Ireland, latest ed., 1985, ed. G. P. and S. P. A. Henderson, published every two years by CBD Research Ltd, 154 High Street, Beckenham, Kent

Encyclopedia of World History, An, 5th ed., by William L. Langer, Harrap, London, 1973

English Historical Documents, ed. D. C. Douglas, 12 vols, in progress (vols 6 and 7 (1558-1660) still to come), Methuen, London

Europa Year Book, 2 vols, published annually by Europa Publications, London

Facts in Focus, Central Statistical Office, Penguin Books in association with HMSO, Harmondsworth, 1972

General Sources of Statistics, by G. F. Lock, Heinemann, London, 1976

Guide to Historical Literature, American Historical Association, Macmillan, New York, 1961

Guide to Historical Periodicals in the English Language, by J. L. Kirby, Historical Association, London, 1970, out of print

Guide to Official Statistics, 4th ed., Central Statistical Office, HMSO, London, 1982

Handbook of British Chronology, new ed., ed. by F. M. Powicke and E. B. Fryde, Royal Historical Society, London, 1985

Handbook of Dates for Students of English History, by C. R. Cheney, Royal Historical Society, London, 1945; latest reprint, 1982

Historical Interpretations, by J. J. Bagley, 2 vols: 1 *Sources of English Medieval History, 1066-1540*; 2 *Sources of English History, 1540 to the Present Day*, David & Charles, Newton Abbot, 1972

Histories of the First and Second World Wars, Government Publications *Sectional List* No. 60, HMSO, London, revised regularly

History, published three times a year by the Historical Association, London

History of England, by G. M. Trevelyan, Longman, London, 1973

History of the English-Speaking Peoples, The, by W. S. Churchill, 4 vols, Cassell, London, 1956-8

History Today, published monthly since 1951, London

Hollis Press & Public Relations Annual, published by Hollis Directories, Sunbury-on-Thames, Middx

How To Find Out: Printed and On-Line Sources, 5th ed., by G. Chandler, Pergamon, Oxford, 1982

Illustrated London News, weekly from May 1842; now monthly, London

Irregular Serials & Annuals: An International Directory, 10th ed., Bowker, New York, 1984

Keesing's Contemporary Archives, published weekly since July 1931, now by Keesing's Publications (Longman), Harlow, Essex

Modern Historians on British History 1485-1945, by G. R. Elton, Methuen, London, 1970

Monthly Digest of Statistics, Central Statistical Office, HMSO, London

New Cambridge Modern History, The, 14 vols, first published by Cambridge University Press, 1957-74 (some vols now revised)

Now I Remember, rev. ed., by Ronald Hamilton, Chatto & Windus, London, 1983; paperback, Hogarth Press, 1984

NUJ Freelance Directory, National Union of Journalists, London, latest ed., 1984

Oxford History of England, The, 15 vols, Clarendon Press, Oxford, 1936-65

Pelican History of England, The, 9 vols, Penguin Books, Harmondsworth, 1950-65

Reviews of United Kingdom Statistical Sources, 5 vols, Heinemann, London, 1974-6

Second World War, The: A Guide to Documents in the Public Record Office, PRO Handbook No. 15, HMSO, London, 1972

Sources in British Political History, 1900-1951, 6 vols, ed. Chris Cook, Macmillan, London, 1975-84

Statesman's Year Book, published annually by Macmillan, London

Tatler & Bystander, first published 1709, now monthly, London

Times Index, first published 1790, now monthly, with annual cumulations, by Research Publications, Reading

Whitaker's Almanack, published annually by J. Whitaker, London

5

Research for Fiction Writers and Dramatists

The amount and depth of research to be undertaken by the writer of fiction will depend upon his choice for the story's setting and the extent of his own knowledge of that setting, and also upon his acquaintance with the kind of people he is writing about. Basically, the research will be concerned with creating an authentic background to the plot and with writing dialogue in the correct idiom. As the problems which face the writer of modern fiction and drama are rather different from those of the writer of historical fiction and drama, they are here examined separately. All that is said about the novel applies equally to the short story and to drama.

The Modern Novel: Background

There is no substitute for a personal visit to every place in which your story, or scene of a story, is to be set. Only through first-hand experience will you absorb the atmosphere of a place, find out exactly how long it will take your character to get from A to B and what buildings or other landmarks he will pass on the way; by using your eyes and ears and nose, by travelling on the local bus, and by spending a few evenings at the pub, you can learn pretty well everything you need to know about the way the locals live, behave and talk. And if you make a point of attending at least once each kind of event that is going to crop up in your story or play – whether it is a boxing match, a race meeting, a sale at Sotheby's, a ballet performance, a court hearing, or anything else – there will probably be little further research that you need to do, beyond the seeking of a few facts and figures to supplement your personal observation.

Inevitably, sometimes, a personal visit is out of the question, and then you have no choice but to rely on second-hand sources. If this is the case, first of all equip yourself with a good, large-scale map or two – preferably a street map of each town in which the action of your story is to take place, as well as a map of the whole district. You can obtain much free information of this nature from town halls or tourist offices.

Travel brochures are always a helpful source, and there are any number of excellent general topographical guides to various regions of the United Kingdom. (How to obtain information on places abroad is dealt with in chapter 9, 'Information from Foreign Sources', pages 124-40). *Whitaker's Almanack* and *Britain: An Official Handbook* each contain a surprising amount of data which will be invaluable for the story or drama set in this country. AA publications such as the *Great Britain Road Atlas* and the *Book of British Towns* are useful for quick reference, while the researcher wishing to find out more about the origin and meaning of place names should consult the *Concise Oxford Dictionary of Place-Names* and the volumes (by county) published by the English Place-Name Society.

If you need to describe particular buildings you will find Nikolaus Pevsner's *Buildings of England* series, also one per county, enormously helpful. In addition, all stately homes and castles open to the public produce their own guidebooks, some more comprehensive and informative than others. Two annual publications, the AA's *Stately Homes, Museums, Castles and Gardens* and the less expensive *Historic Houses, Castles and Gardens in Great Britain and Ireland* carry brief details of all such properties. The curators of these historic houses are usually well-informed, but may be too busy to talk to you on days when the public is admitted; a telephone call or preliminary letter beforehand may well lead to a special appointment and personally guided tour, with much additional information.

Other essential reference tools are railway and bus time-tables of the area you are describing: these will (or should) save you from making an elementary mistake such as putting a character on the train at the wrong London terminus or misjudging the time taken for a particular journey.

An excellent way to get the 'feel' of a place, when it is not possible for you to visit it, is to take out a subscription to the local newspaper and county magazine; you will find lists of these, under towns, in both *Benn's Media Directory* and *Willing's Press Guide* (see chapter 3, 'Basic Sources of Information', page 39).

People

Often the background to a story or play will concern a particular profession or industry, and here too the best method of research is to mix as much as possible with people in the field. The secretary of the relevant professional or trade association (check names and addresses in the current *Directory of British Associations and Associations in Ireland,* in the *Trade Associations and Professional Bodies of the United Kingdom,* in the *Hollis Press & Public Relations Annual,* or in *Whitaker's Almanack* – see chapter 4, pages 59-60) will usually be very helpful if you do not have any personal contacts, and most large corporations or companies have a press and public relations department or member of staff who will assist you. You should not feel diffident about approaching such people; it is rare for a genuine request for information to be refused point blank, and very often the enquirer will be invited to visit a factory or training establishment or to attend as an observer one or two meetings of the relevant society – all this is grist to the mill. Nevertheless, it is unfair to impinge too much on someone else's time or expertise – even if this is being paid for by his company – and so a luncheon or dinner invitation is a nice gesture. An incredible amount can be learned from an hour's conversation face to face.

Much of what has been said about background research also applies to finding out about people, for there is nothing better than to spend time with whatever age, regional, or occupational group the writer wishes to bring into his story. It is essential to observe at first-hand how people behave, talk and dress. Every writer should try, therefore, to cultivate a wide circle of friends in all walks of life, and the fiction writer especially will do well to get to know a psychologist with whom he can discuss the actions and reactions of his characters, as well as a doctor with whom he can verify medical symptoms and treatments. The crime writer ought to be on friendly terms with at least one member of the police force who is willing to put him right on procedures and jargon; only as a last resort should he telephone or write to New Scotland Yard (where, however, if he has a genuine problem an information officer will usually help). For all writers of crime and detective fiction access to copies of *Moriarty's Police Law,* or the more recent *Butterworth's Police Law,* and Keith Simpson's *Forensic Medicine* is indispensable.

When reliance must be placed on documentary sources, a careers pamphlet or training manual for the relevant trade or profession will yield a good deal of information. The memoirs and diaries of eminent people in that trade or profession should be looked at, and also the appropriate in-house or trade journals, for these will all provide up-to-date material and jargon, and sometimes also historical detail.

So far as the behaviour of your characters are concerned, personal observation may be supplemented by a simple textbook on psychology or behavioural study, such as those published by Penguin

Books. Desmond Morris has written two fascinating studies, *Manwatching* and *Gestures*, illustrating all kinds of gestures, signals and actions that people make and their interpretation, which are of interest to all writers.

Two useful sources of information on nicknames (both modern and historical) are the *Handbook of Pseudonyms and Personal Nicknames* compiled by H. Sharp, and the *Pseudonyms and Nicknames Dictionary* published by Gale Research of Detroit, USA.

Language

It is highly dangerous for the writer who is unfamiliar with a foreign language, local dialect or occupational slang to dabble in these fields, but if he must do so he should always try to get what he has written verified by an expert. So far as English is concerned, useful works to be found in most reference libraries include the 4-volume *Survey of English Dialects* by H. Orton and E. Dieth, and the *English Dialect Dictionary* by J. Wright.

There are a number of so-called 'slang dictionaries', and these have their uses. However, since it is necessary first to know the word or expression whose meaning you wish to look up in them, their value must be limited. Of far greater value to the novelist or dramatist, therefore, is Eric Partridge's *Slang Today and Yesterday*, which has separate sections dealing with slang spoken in chronological periods and in various occupational groups. Mr Partridge also compiled a *Dictionary of the Underworld, British and American*, which will serve the crime writer well (although this too is arranged as a dictionary), and also a fascinating *Dictionary of Catch Phrases* (British and American), from the 16th century to the present day. An up-to-date work is Jonathan Green's *Newspeak: A Dictionary of Jargon*. Among other valuable books on the subject, *Sea Slang of the 20th Century* by W. Granville covers the language of yachtsmen, fishermen, bargemen and all naval personnel.

The children's writer will find P. Opie's *The Lore and Language of Schoolchildren* very helpful, and also J. S. Butcher's *Greyfriars School Prospectus*, which contains a glossary of school slang and expressions used by Frank Richards in the 'Billy Bunter' books. However, it cannot be stressed too strongly that language is changing all the time – and especially the language of the young – so that there is no substitute for the writer mixing with, and talking and listening to, the younger generation, in order to get the idiom exactly right.

Quite often a writer is at a loss to know how one of his characters would address another, perhaps someone in an elevated position.

Here either *Debrett's Correct Form* or *Titles and Forms of Address* will provide the answer, supplying as a bonus a guide to practically every situation likely to arise, socially and professionally, including American usage. These books will also be invaluable for the researcher wishing to know how to write or talk to titled or official persons whom he needs to contact for information.

The Historical Novel

The writer of an historical novel must be thoroughly familiar with the period in which his story is set, and especially knowledgeable about the manners, customs and daily life of the people concerned. He must also be accurate about major events and prominent people. This will not present any great difficulty so long as he keeps at his elbow as he works a general bibliography and authoritative history of the period, as well as a good biographical dictionary (suggested titles are mentioned in chapter 4, 'Historical Research' (pages 57-65) and chapter 6, 'Biography' (pages 84-102)).

It is of the utmost importance to use contemporary sources wherever possible, and you should make good use of the *English Historical Documents* series. Also recommended are the *They Saw It Happen* and the *Human Documents* series; some of these are now out of print, but they will be found in most reference libraries. G. M. Trevelyan's *English Social History* remains one of the best general accounts of life in this country through the ages, while the lifestyle of the upper classes is admirably portrayed in Mark Girouard's *Life in the English Country House*. R. Graves' and A. Hodges' *The Long Week-End* is very evocative of the years between the two world wars, and it has recently become available again. The *Pelican Social History of Britain*, the first volume of which appeared in 1982, is also worth collecting. In addition, there are a number of excellent encyclopedias and social histories devoted to particular periods – Madeleine S. and J. Lane Miller's *Encyclopedia of Bible Life*, for example, or, on English life, studies such as E. N. Williams, *Life in Georgian England*, Dorothy Marshall's *English People in the 18th Century*, J. H. Plumb's *Georgian Delights*, John Fisher's *The World of the Forsytes*, and Norman Longmate's *How We Lived Then: A History of Everyday Life during the Second World War*, to mention but a few. G. D. H. Cole and R. Postgate's *The Common People 1746-1938* has become a standard work; see also *The Common People: A History from the Norman Conquest to the Present*, by J. F. C. Harrison. In lighter vein, but very informative, are C. L. Graves' *Mr Punch's History of Modern England*, covering the years from 1841 to 1914, and Leslie Baily's *BBC Scrapbooks 1896-1939*. Alan

Jenkins has written two excellent studies of the 20th century, *The Thirties* and *The Forties*.

Autobiographies and diaries are extremely useful as source-material for the historical novelist in that they provide absolutely authentic accounts of day-to-day life and thought of the period, written in the contemporary idiom. In William Matthews' *British Diaries 1442-1942* and in John Stuart Batts' *British Manuscript Diaries of the 19th Century* the diaries are listed under the year in which they commence, which enables the researcher to see what material exists for a particular period. *British Autobiographies*, also compiled by William Matthews, is an annotated bibliography of material published or written before 1951. The same author has compiled an annotated bibliography of *American Diaries* written prior to 1861 and also *American Diaries in Manuscript 1580-1954*. See also *American Diaries: an annotated bibliography of published American diaries and journals*, published by Gale Research, Detroit, and another US publication, edited by T. P. Riggio, *American Diaries 1902-1926*.

Most public libraries have a local collection, and you should always ask if there is a book dealing with a particular region, town, industry or local family, in the period about which you are writing. (For further suggestions, see chapter 7, 'Family and Local History' pages 103-118.)

One good method of keeping the story of an historical novel or play in line with world or national events is to refer constantly to a published chronology. There are a number to choose from, such as the series published originally by Barrie & Rockcliff/Barrie & Jenkins: *Chronology of the Ancient World* (BC-799 AD); *Chronology of the Medieval World* (800-1491); *Chronology of the Expanding World* (1492-1762); and *Chronology of the Modern World* (1763-1965). In these volumes the major events of each year are listed month by month, while also included are annual listings of the developments in the arts, sciences, politics, etc., together with the births and deaths of famous people.

Problems likely to be encountered by the writer of historical fiction and some suggestions as to how they may be solved are discussed below.

Places

Many of the places and buildings you may want to mention in your novel or play still exist today, but have changed out of all recognition in the last few hundred years, and it is not easy to find out exactly how they looked at a particular date. You should always ask at the local library or record office if they have maps of approximately the right date, and where these exist you will find it valuable to keep a photocopy of the map in front of you as you write. There is an historical series of the Ordnance Survey, which may be useful, and you can buy reprints of the first (one-inch) edition. A good historical atlas – *Newnes Historical Atlas* or the *Penguin Atlas of World History* are recommended – is essential, or you may prefer to have one of the three inexpensive Penguin atlases, *Ancient History*, *Medieval History* or *Recent History*.

Like the writer of modern fiction, the historical novelist should try to visit every place or building that comes into his story. If this is quite impossible, the best course is to enquire at your local library or county record office for a reliable parish history and for any books about life in the district during the period in which you are interested, as, for example, Edward Hughes' *North Country Life in the 18th Century* or William Addison's *Essex Heyday*; there are many more. If your story is set in the 18th century or later, you will be able to study the local newspaper. Where buildings have to be described, Nikolaus Pevsner's *Buildings of England* series, already mentioned, will be most useful; also H. M. Colvin's *History of the King's Works*. For buildings in London, there is the very detailed *Survey of London*. Other useful sources are the guidebooks to historic castles and houses open to the public. Isabel Quigly's *The Heirs of Tom Brown*, with its excellent bibliography, will help you if you are setting part of your story in a public school.

Dates

The problems that arise over dating have been discussed in the previous chapter. In historical fiction work the writer will most often need to find out on what day of the week a certain anniversary or religious festival fell. This can be done very easily by first looking up the date of Easter in the chronological table at the back of the *Handbook of Dates for Students of English History* and then by turning to the appropriate calendar section, in which there is a double-page spread for all the years from AD 500 to 2000 in which Easter fell (or is going to fall) on that particular day. In the same *Handbook* you will find a list of saints' days and religious festivals, but if you need more detail on festivals you should consult the *British Calendar Customs* series published by the Folklore Society.

Weather

What the weather was like on a certain day, or if a particular winter was severe, or when there was a heatwave and how long it lasted, can be vital to an historical novel. *Whitaker's Almanack* (from 1868) is a good source, and so are local and regional newspapers. *The Times* has employed a regular weather correspondent since the early 1870s, but earlier reports – from 1731 – appeared in *Gentleman's Magazine*, where you will find not only monthly tables giving temperatures and rainfall, but a calendar with brief descriptions against each day, such as 'cloudy morning, but bright later'; 'windy and wet all day'; 'heavy rain in the south, snow in the north'.

Two excellent works which are rare books and to be found nowadays only at the major libraries are T. H. Baker's *Records of the Seasons, etc. . . . observed in the British Isles* and E. J. Lowe's *Natural Phenomena and Chronology of the Seasons* (of which Part I only was ever published, containing records from AD 220 to 1753). Among other useful reference books are D. Bowen's *Britain's Weather*, which has an appendix listing notable gales, blizzards, floods and frosts; J. H. Brazell's *London Weather*, with its useful chronology from AD 4 to 1964; and W. Andrews' *Famous Frosts and Frost Fairs in Great Britain*. For information about the weather in different regions of the globe, the best source is W. G. Kendrew's *The Climates of the Continents*.

In England, the Meteorological Office has published records since the 1860s. Its Library and Archives Department contains many earlier records, covering the entire world; researchers are allowed to use the Library, and in special cases books will be loaned by post. The Librarian will usually recommend titles or will pass a specific query on to the Climate Branch, who may charge a modest fee if extensive research has to be undertaken by staff. Enquiries should be addressed in the first instance to the National Meteorological Library, London Road, Bracknell, Berks RG12 2SZ (tel. Bracknell (0344) 420242).

Language

Getting the idiom right in historical fiction is often a big worry to the writer. The best advice that can be given is that he should read extensively the best novels and plays of the relevant age; by so doing, he will gradually acquire the 'feel' of the spoken English of the time. The meanings of words can be checked in the big *Oxford English Dictionary*, in the *Shorter OED*, or in the *Routledge Dictionary of Historical Slang*. Eric Partridge's *Slang Today and Yesterday*, as mentioned earlier in this chapter, has useful sections on the slang spoken at different periods (16th to 20th centuries inclusive). If you are setting your story in the last war, you should look at *The Language of World War II*, which covers not only spoken expressions but also the slogans and abbreviations then current, as well as the popular songs of the time.

Cost of living, currencies and wages

How much people earned and what they paid for their food and clothing are queries that frequently crop up in historical writing. J. Burnett's *A History of the Cost of Living* will answer most needs: it has chapters dating from the Middle Ages to the present day, and also a good bibliography. Another exceptionally informative source is the *What It Cost the Day Before Yesterday Book* by Harold Priestley, which is divided into three periods: 1851-1914, 1915-1970 and (to take account of recent inflation) 1971-1978. *Prices and Wages in England from the 12th to the 19th Century* by Lord Beveridge and others is a standard work, and Peter Wilsher's *The Pound in your Pocket 1870-1970* is a very readable and well-researched study of the pound and its purchasing power over the last hundred years. Newspapers and women's magazines are valuable sources from the early 19th century onwards – advertisements as much as text – while for a general survey A. Adburgham's *Shops and Shopping 1800-1914* is excellent. *Edwardian Shopping* and *Yesterday's Shopping*, reprinted from the Army and Navy Stores' catalogues of 1898-1913 and 1907 respectively, provide a record both of changing fashion and of prices at that time.

Currency Conversion Tables: A Hundred Years of Change by R. L. Bidwell is a most useful guide to the fluctuations in rates of exchange of most countries of the world since 1870; it also has a table of London gold prices. For money values in earlier times there is Peter Spufford's recent *Handbook of Medieval Exchange*. If you should need other historical information or monetary rates, it is best to write or telephone to the Bank of England Information Division, Threadneedle Street, London EC2R 8AH (tel. 01-601 4444).

Fashion, etiquette and food

The standard work on English costume is the series by C. W. and P. E. Cunnington, which consists of *Handbooks* covering the medieval period and the 16th, 17th, 18th, 19th and 20th centuries in separate volumes. For quick reference there is the *Dictionary of English Costume 900-1900* by C. W. and P. E. Cunnington and Charles Beard. Also useful is *The Evolution of Fashion: Pattern and Cut from 1066 to 1930* by M. Hamilton Hill and Peter Bucknell, while Alison Lurie's recent study, *The Language of Clothes*, is both a thoroughly researched and witty comment on dress and manners that will help both the modern and the historical novelist. Other titles are listed in the booklet *Costume: A General Bibliography*, published by the Costume Society. On hairdressing there is R.

Corson's *Fashions in Hair: the first 5000 Years*, R. Turner Wilcox's *The Mode in Hats and Headdress* (from ancient Egyptian to the present day) and G. de Courtais' *Women's Headdress and Hairstyles in England from* AD *600 to the Present Day*.

The best guides to English manners and etiquette are J. Wildeblood and P. Brinson's *The Polite World* (covering the 13th to the 19th centuries) and *A Punch History of Manners 1841-1940*, by A. Adburgham. On eating habits and diet there are Arnold Palmer's *Movable Feasts*, G. Brett's *Dinner is Served*, J. C. Drummond and A. Wilbraham's *Englishman's Food: Five Centuries of English Diet*, and J. Burnett's *Plenty and Want: A Social History of Diet in England from 1815 to the Present Day*.

Transport and travel

One of the best general studies is E. A. Pratt's *History of Inland Transport and Communications*. David & Charles of Newton Abbot, Devon, are publishers who specialise in railway and transport history, and it is worth asking for their current catalogue and stocklist. Finding out exactly how long a particular journey would have taken at a particular date is not easy, but so far as train journeys are concerned it is a good idea to look at an early Bradshaw (first published in 1839) or at the time-table nearest in date to that used in the story. Stage-coach time-tables will be found in the early London directories.

Finding out about Published Fiction

In addition to the specific research problems connected with his own work, the fiction writer or playwright frequently wants to know what other novels or plays or short stories have been published with similar themes or backgrounds. He may also wish to check on whether any other writer has used the title which he has in mind. (There is no copyright in titles, but for the exact legal position, see the Society of Authors' *Quick Guide* on the *Protection of Titles*.)

Most public libraries possess copies of the *Fiction Index*, the *Play Index* and the *Short Story Index*; you should ask for them at the readers' enquiry desk. To date there are four cumulated *Fiction Index* volumes, covering 1945-60, 1960-69, 1970-74 and 1975-79 respectively; since 1970 the *Index* has been published annually in the spring following the year indexed. Titles are listed under some 3,000 subject headings.

The latest volume of the *Short Story Index* brings it up to 1983, and there is a single volume of *Collections Indexed 1900-1978*. There are six volumes of the *Play Index*, covering the period 1949-1982; synopses of the plots of plays are included, together with an author, title and subject listing.

The writer wishing to find out about historical fiction published before 1929 should consult J. Nield's *Guide to the Best Historical Novels and Tales*; another useful select bibliography (unfortunately now out of print) is the Historical Association's *Historical Novels*.

American Diaries: an annotated bibliography of American diaries written prior to year 1861, by William Matthews, University of California Press, Berkeley and Los Angeles, 1945, 1959

American Diaries: an annotated bibliography of published American diaries and journals, by L. Arksey, N. Pries and M. Reed, Gale Research, Detroit, 1983

American Diaries in Manuscript, 1580-1954, by William Matthews, University of Georgia Press, Athens, 1974

American Diaries 1902-1926, ed. T. P. Riggio, University of Pennsylvania Press, Philadelphia, 1982

BBC Scrapbooks, by Leslie Baily, 2 vols: I, *1896-1914*; II, *1918-1939*, Allen & Unwin, London, 1966-68

Benn's Media Directory, published annually by Benn Business Information Services Ltd., Tonbridge, Kent

Book of British Towns, Automobile Association, Basingstoke, 1979

Britain: An Official Handbook, published annually by HMSO, London

Britain's Weather, by David Bowen, David & Charles, Newton Abbot, 1969

British Autobiographies: an annotated bibliography of British autobiographies published or written before 1951, by William Matthews, University of California Press, Berkeley and Los Angeles, 1955

British Calendar Customs: England, 3 vols, 1936-40; *Scotland*, 3 vols, 1939-41; *Orkneys and Shetland*, 1946, published by The Folklore Society, London

British Diaries 1442-1942: an annotated bibliography of British diaries written between 1442 and 1942, by William Matthews, University of California Press, Berkeley and Los Angeles, 1950

British Manuscript Diaries of the 19th Century: an annotated listing, by John Stuart Batts, Centaur Press, Fontwell and London, 1976

Butterworth's Police Law, Butterworth, London, 1985

Buildings of England, edited by N. Pevsner, 46 vols, 1951 onwards; Penguin Books, Harmondsworth, revised editions in progress

Chronology of the Ancient World, BC-799 AD, by H. E. L. Mellersh, Barrie & Jenkins, London, 1976

Chronology of the Medieval World, 800-1491, by R. L. Storey, Barrie & Rockcliff, London, 1973

Chronology of the Expanding World, 1492-1762, by N. Williams, Barrie & Rockcliff, London, 1969

Chronology of the Modern World, 1763-1965, by N. Williams, Barrie & Rockcliff, London, 1966; paperback, Penguin Books, 1975

Climates of the Continents, The, 5th ed., by W. G. Kendrew, Clarendon Press, Oxford, 1961

Common People, The, 1746-1938, by G. D. H. Cole and R. Postgate, Methuen, London, 1938; reprinted 1965

Common People, The: A History from the Norman Conquest to the Present, by J. F. C. Harrison, Fontana, London, 1984

Concise Oxford Dictionary of Place-Names, 4th ed., compiled by E. Ekwall, Clarendon Press, Oxford, 1960; reprinted 1974

Costume: A General Bibliography, by P. Anthony and J. Arnold, published by The Costume Society, London; latest edition 1974 (new ed. in preparation)

Currency Conversion Tables: A Hundred Years of Change, by R. L. Bidwell, Rex Collings, London, 1970

Debrett's Correct Form, rev. ed., Debrett's Peerage/Country Life/ Futura, London, 1976; paperback, 1979

Dictionary of Catch Phrases, British and American, from the Sixteenth Century to the Present Day, new ed., by Eric Partridge, Routledge, London, 1985

Dictionary of English Costume 900-1900, by C. W. and P. E. Cunnington and Charles Beard, A & C Black, London, 1960; reprinted 1976

Dictionary of the Underworld: British and American, 3rd ed. rev., by Eric Partridge, Routledge, London, 1968

Dinner is Served, by G. Brett, Hart-Davis, London, 1968

Directory of British Associations and Associations in Ireland, latest ed., 1985, ed. G. P. and S. P. A. Henderson, published by C.B.D. Research Ltd, 154 High Street, Beckenham, Kent BR3 1EA, every two years

Edwardian Shopping: A Selection from the Army & Navy Stores Catalogue 1898-1913, compiled by R. H. Langbridge, David & Charles, Newton Abbot, 1975

Encyclopedia of Bible Life, rev. ed., by Madeleine S. and J. Lane Miller, A & C Black, London, 1979

English Dialect Dictionary, by J. Wright, Frowde, London, 1898-1905; new ed., Oxford University Press, Oxford, 1981

English Historical Documents, ed. D. C. Douglas, covering *c*. 500-1914, 12 vols., (vols 6 and 7 (1558-1660) still in progress), Methuen, London

English People of the 18th Century, by Dorothy Marshall, Longman, London, 1956

English Place-Name Society, volumes by county, in progress since 1924, published by the Society, c/o University of Nottingham

English Social History, new ed., by G. M. Trevelyan, Longman, London, 1978; paperback, Penguin Books

Englishman's Food, The: A History of Five Centuries of English Diet, new ed., by J. C. Drummond and A. Wilbraham, Cape, London, 1958

Essex Heyday, by William Addison, Dent, London, 1949

Evolution of Fashion: Pattern and Cut from 1066 to 1930, by M. Hamilton Hill and P. Bucknell, Batsford, London, 1967

Famous Frosts and Frost Fairs in Great Britain, by W. Andrews, Redway, London, 1887

Fashions in Hair: The First 5000 Years, by R. Corson, Peter Owen, London, 1965

Fiction Index, published annually by the Association of Assistant Librarians, London, since 1970; cumulated vols *1945-60*, 1961; *1960-69*, 1970; *1970-74*, 1975; *1975-1979*, 1980; *1980-84*, 1985

Forensic Medicine, 9th ed., by Keith Simpson, E. Arnold, London, 1985

Forties, The, by Alan Jenkins, Heinemann, London, 1976

Gentleman's Magazine, 1731-1922; there are several general index volumes and a 2-vol index to biographical and obituary notices 1731-1819 (see page 52)

Georgian Delights, by J. H. Plumb, Weidenfeld & Nicolson, London, 1980

Gestures: Their Origins and Distribution, by Desmond Morris, Cape, London, 1979; paperback, Triad, 1981

Great Britain Road Atlas, Automobile Association, Basingstoke, revised regularly

Greyfriars School Prospectus, by J. S. Butcher, Cassell, London, 1965

Guide to the Best Historical Novels and Tales, 5th ed., by J. Nield, Matthews, London, 1929

Handbook of English Costume series, by C. W. and P. E. Cunnington, Faber, London, 1952-73; progressively revised editions

Handbook of Dates for Students of English History, ed. C. R. Cheney, Royal Historical Society, London, 1945; latest reprint, 1982

Handbook of Medieval Exchange, by Peter Spufford, Royal Historical Society, London, 1985

Handbook of Pseudonyms and Personal Nicknames, 2 vols, compiled by Harold S. Sharp, Scarecrow, Metuchen, NJ, 1972; supplements, 1975, 1982

Heirs of Tom Brown, The, by Isabel Quigly, Chatto & Windus, London, 1982; paperback, Oxford University Press, 1984

Historic Houses, Castles and Gardens in Great Britain and Ireland, published annually by British Leisure Publications, East Grinstead, W. Sussex

Historical Novels, by Helen Cam, Historical Association, London, 1961; reprinted, 1974

History of Inland Transport and Communication, by E. A. Pratt, 1912; reprinted, 1970, David & Charles, Newton Abbot

History of the Cost of Living, A, by John Burnett, Penguin Books, Harmondsworth, 1969

History of the King's Works, The, ed. H. M. Colvin, HMSO, London, 1963-, still in progress

Hollis Press & Public Relations Annual, published by Hollis Directories, Sunbury-on-Thames, Middx

How We Lived Then: A History of Everyday Life during the Second World War, by N. Longmate, Hutchinson, London, 1971; paperback, Arrow, 1977

Human Documents series, by R. E. Pike, Allen & Unwin, London. The volumes are (latest editions in brackets, some out of print): *Human Documents of the Industrial Revolution in Britain* (1978); *of Adam Smith's Time* (1973); *of the Victorian Golden Age* (1967); *of the Age of the Forsytes* (1970); *of the Lloyd George Era* (1972)

Language of Clothes, The, by Alison Lurie, Heinemann, London, 1982; paperback ed., Hamlyn, 1983

Language of World War II, H. W. Wilson, New York, 1948

Life in the English Country House, by Mark Girouard, Yale University Press, New York and London, 1978; paperback Penguin Books, 1980

Life in Georgian England, by E. N. Williams, Batsford, London, 1962

London Weather, by J. H. Brazell, HMSO, London, 1968

Long Week-end, The: A Social History of Great Britain 1918-1939, by Robert Graves and Alan Hodge, Hutchinson, London, 1985

Lore and Language of Schoolchilrden, The, by P. Opie, Clarendon Press, Oxford, 1959; paperback, Paladin, 1977

Manwatching: A Field Guide to Human Behaviour, by Desmond Morris, Cape, London, 1977; paperback, Triad/Panther, 1978

Mr Punch's History of Modern England, 4 vols, by C. L. Graves, Cassell, London, 1921-2

Modes in Hats and Headdress, rev. ed., by R. Turner Wilcox, Scribner's, New York, 1959

Moriarty's Police Law, 24th ed., Butterworth, London, 1981

Movable Feasts: Changes in English Eating-Habits, by Arnold Palmer, Oxford University Press paperback, 1984

Natural Phenomena and Chronology of the Seasons, by E. J. Lowe, Part I only, London, 1870

Newspeak: A Dictionary of Jargon, by Jonathan Green, Routledge, London, 1984; paperback, 1985

Newnes Historical Atlas (originally the *Hamlyn Historical Atlas*), rev. ed., Newnes, London, 1983

North Country Life in the 18th Century, by Edward Hughes, Oxford University Press, Oxford, 1952

Ordnance Survey, first edition reprinted by David & Charles, Newton Abbot; modern editions, HMSO/Ordnance Survey, London and Southampton

Oxford English Dictionary, 13 vols, Clarendon Press, Oxford, 1884-1928; with three supplements, 1972-82; compact edition with reading glass, 2 vols, 1971; also *Shorter OED*, 3rd ed., reset, 2 vols, 1973

Pelican Social History of Britain, Penguin Books, Harmondsworth, 4 vols to date, 1982-, in progress

Penguin Atlas of Ancient History, by C. McEvedy, Penguin Books, Harmondworth, 1970

Penguin Atlas of Medieval History, by C. McEvedy, Penguin Books, Harmondsworth, 1979

Penguin Atlas of Recent History: Europe since 1815, Penguin Books, Harmondsworth, 1982

Penguin Atlas of World History, 2 vols, translated from German by H. Kinder and W. Hilgemann, Penguin Books, Harmondsworth, 1974; reprinted 1984

Play Index, published by H. W. Wilson, New York, since 1953. Six vols to date: 1949-1952; 1953-1960; 1961-1967; 1968-1972; 1973-1977; 1978-1982

Plenty and Want: A Social History of Diet in England from 1815 to the Present Day, by John Burnett, Methuen, London, 1978

Polite World, The: A Guide to English Manners and Deportment from the 13th to the 19th Century, rev. ed., by J. Wildeblood and P. Brinson, Oxford University Press, 1974

Pound in Your Pocket 1870-1970, The, by Peter Wilsher, Cassell, London, 1970

Prices and Wages in England from the 12th to the 19th Century, by Lord Beveridge and others, Frank Cass, London, 1965

Protection of Titles, a Society of Authors *Quick Guide*, available to non-members from the Society, 84 Drayton Gardens, London SW10 9SD, price £1 post free (UK)

Pseudonyms and Nicknames Dictionary, 2nd ed., ed. Jennifer Mossman, Gale Research, Detroit, 1982

Punch History of Manners 1841-1940, A, by A. Adburgham, Hutchinson, London, 1961

Records of Seasons and Prices of Agricultural Produce & Phenomena observed in the British Isles, by T. H. Baker, Simpkin Marshall, London, 1883

Routledge Dictionary of Historical Slang, Routledge, London, 1973

Sea Slang of the 20th Century, by W. Granville, Winchester Publications, 1949

Shops and Shopping, 2nd ed., by A. Adburgham, Allen & Unwin, London, 1981

Short Story Index, published by H. W. Wilson, New York, since 1953. Basic volume 1900-1949; supplementary vols to 1974. Since 1974 published annually with 5-yearly cumulations (latest vol 1979-1983); also a single volume of *Collections Indexed 1900-1978*

Slang Today and Yesterday, 4th ed., by Eric Partridge, Routledge, London, 1970

Stately Homes, Museums, Castles and Gardens in Britain, Automobile Association, Basingstoke, annually

Survey of English Dialects, by H. Orton and E. Dieth, E. J. Arnold, Leeds, introduction and 4 regional vols, 1962-70

Survey of English Place-Names, see infra, English Place-Name Society

Survey of London, LCC, now by Athlone Press, London, for the GLC, 41 vols to date, 1900-, continuing

They Saw It Happen, series, 4 vols covering 55 BC-1940, Blackwell, Oxford, 1973; now out of print

Thirties, The, by Alan Jenkins, Heinemann, London, 1976

Titles and Forms of Address: A Guide to Correct Use, 18th ed., A & C Black, London, 1985

Trade Associations and Professional Bodies of the United Kingdom, 7th ed., by P. Millard, Pergamon, Oxford, 1984

What It Cost the Day before Yesterday Book, by H. Priestley, Kenneth Mason, Emsworth, 1979

Whitaker's Almanack, published annually by J. Whitaker, London

Willing's Press Guide, published annually by Thomas Skinner Directories, East Grinstead, W. Sussex

Women's Headdress and Hairstyles in England from AD *600 to Present Day*, by G. de Courtais, Batsford, London, 1973
Yesterday's Shopping, reprinted catalogue of the Army & Navy Stores 1907, David & Charles, Newton Abbot, 1969

6

Biography

Biographical writing may consist of a short article on a celebrity, past or present, to be published perhaps in commemoration of a centenary or an 80th birthday, or it may be a full-length study. It sometimes happens that a book grows out of the research undertaken for a newspaper or magazine article. Occasionally biographies are written of people who during their lifetime were not especially renowned or eminent, but whose papers (usually diaries or letters) make a unique contribution to the social history of their time.

There is a growing trend for biographies to be written while their subjects are still alive, or very soon after their death; this may have something to do with the fear of the modern biographer that once the biographee and his contemporaries have gone, there may be little material to work on, seeing that letter-writing is a dying art and telephoning an increasing convenience. The academic view of such work, however, is that it constitutes a 'study' or 'profile' of the person concerned rather than a true biography, and that while the study or profile as such may be of inestimable value to a future biographer, it is essential for a certain amount of time to have elapsed before any life can be properly evaluated and seen in perspective to its time.

The author who embarks on a biographical project normally has some good reason for wanting to write it – kinship to the subject, or an intimate working relationship with him or her, and/or the possession of – and access to – original papers. Or, if a number of 'lives' have already been published on the person concerned, the writer may simply have a burning desire to write from a fresh angle, to 'set the record straight' or to throw new light on some controversial aspects as a result of recent research. It is generally accepted that the famous characters of history will stand new biographies every ten years.

Whatever the motive, it is advisable to try to get the work commissioned and – especially where a full-length book is envisaged – to secure a cash advance, for there will be a considerable amount of

83

research to be undertaken and expenses to be met. In calculating the likely total costs, you should not forget to take into account your own working time. Out-of-pocket expenditure will include travel, meals away from home, postal and telephone charges, photocopying, photographs and stationery, at the very least; there may well be 'extras' such as library search fees, fees payable to a genealogist or research assistant, the cost of professional typing and indexing, reproduction fees for illustrations, and so on.

Before a publisher signs a contract, or parts with any money to a writer who is unknown to him, he will normally ask to see a synopsis, or maybe even a chapter or two, of the proposed work. The research that has to be done for the purposes of writing this synopsis is roughly the same as what would be needed for a short biographical article: both must include the salient points of the life and mention the existence of any hitherto unpublished material and/or recent research that provide a new angle. It must be done in sufficient depth so as to convince the potential publisher that the book will be a good investment.

The writer who has reached this stage is bound to be familiar with the outline life of his subject. However, it may not be out of place to record here, as an *aide-mémoire*, the main sources open to biographers and to researchers seeking biographical information for use in other work.

The importance of researching 'in the round' has been stressed earlier in this handbook. In biographical research this is particularly important. It is essential to uncover the whole person, 'warts and all', so that at the research stage nothing should be avoided or glossed over or left unexplored. Motives for a person's actions may be discussed in the final work, and whether the biographer writes from a more or a less sympathetic angle is a matter of interpretation rather than one of research: this is a decision each individual writer must make once he has satisfied himself as to the true facts.

Private Papers

One good reason for allowing a certain amount of time to elapse before writing a biography is that there may not be access to private papers for a given number of years after a person's death; although the writer may have possession of his subject's own papers and the blessing of the family concerned to make use of them, it is very probable that some of the material required will be contained in the papers of others and that this may be subject to restrictions. Papers deposited in record offices and other archives are normally subject to the 30-year closure rule or, exceptionally, to an even longer period; in many cases permission will be needed from the family or the estate before the documents may be seen. Although the copyright of correspondence belongs to the writer, the actual letters belong to the recipient or to his heirs or executors, from whom permission must be obtained for access; in practice, unless there is some good reason to the contrary, this is usually forthcoming – but it may be stipulated that the text of the biography must be submitted before going to press. It is important always to make due acknowledgment to the source of such material and to comply with any request for prior submission of the text.

It is true that modern biographies *are* often written without the permission of the subject's family and thus without access to the private papers, but a writer who decides to embark on such a work should be fully aware beforehand of the difficulties that can arise. Quite apart from missing out on material and close family recollections and anecdotes, it may be less easy to obtain other people's help (there is no doubt that when seeking interviews or writing for information, magic phrases such as 'the official biography', 'sanctioned by the family', and so on, *do* carry weight and often swing the balance in the biographer's favour where someone is hesitant about supplying information). More serious can be the reaction of relatives to an 'unofficial' biography, with the possibility that if they are seriously displeased they may seek an injunction through the courts.

The location of unpublished source material in general has been discussed in an earlier chapter (see pages 45-50). For the biographer needing to find out whether any private papers exist and, if so, their whereabouts, the first point of call must be the National Register of Archives, maintained by the Royal Commission on Historical Manuscripts at Quality House, Quality Court, Chancery Lane, London WC2A 1HP; enquiries should be made in person or in writing, not by telephone. By using the highly efficient catalogue and cross-referenced indexing system, the researcher will be able to find out the precise location of correspondence and other papers on his subject.

The Department of Manuscripts in the British Library Reference Division and the Public Record Office are both major sources, while the National Maritime Museum at Greenwich has a comparatively recent manuscript collection of interest to the naval biographer. Many universities have important holdings. The Churchill College Archives Centre at Cambridge is collecting papers of 20th-century politicians, scientists, military and naval commanders. The *Guide to the Papers of British Cabinet Ministers 1900-1951*, published by the Royal Historical Society, is a valuable reference tool for the modern biographical researcher. Use should also be made of the 'General Index to Collections' at the back of *British Archives: A Guide to Archive Resources in the United Kingdom*.

The papers of lesser known persons are more difficult to track down. If you are not in touch with the family or cannot trace any relatives, and the local record office has no deposited papers, you may be able to trace executors or other persons likely to be in possession of a deceased person's papers through a Will at Somerset House (see chapter 7 on 'Family and Local History'). If you are writing a biography of someone who lived in the last fifty years, even if you do have access to family and private papers, an advertisement in the national or local press is to be recommended: many unexpected and valuable 'fish' are netted in this way, in the shape of replies from friends, teachers, colleagues, employees and others who have known or met the subject at some period of his life, and may well produce fascinating and very usable factual or anecdotal material of which you would otherwise remain unaware.

It is important to remember that the papers of even the most eminent public personages contain a certain amount of correspondence from people in lesser walks of life, and if you have reason to believe that the subject of your biography had dealings with someone whose papers have been catalogued and/or deposited, do not overlook this source. When researching for biographical information on professional people, it is always worth contacting the librarian or archivist of the relevant society or institution; some of these bodies hold collections of important private papers and most have biographical information that you may not find easily elsewhere, going back to the date of their foundation.

'Private papers' in this context are not limited to correspondence, but may consist of almost any kind of documentary material, such as account books, scrapbooks and photograph albums, visitors' books, personal diaries, and so on.

Printed and Other Sources

Biographical dictionaries

The major source of biographical information on nationals of this country is the *Dictionary of National Biography*, known to scholars, librarians and researchers as 'the *DNB*'. In the current edition there are 22 volumes containing entries in alphabetical sequence for the period up to 1900, and for the 20th century one volume per decade, the latest available being that for 1961 – 70. Few private individuals can afford either the shelf space or the cost (£650) of the complete set, and the 2-volume micrographically reduced compact edition, marketed a few years ago, is no longer obtainable. However, the *Concise DNB*, in two volumes (£35 and £17.50 respectively), is a reference tool that should have a place on every writer's bookshelf: it contains brief entries for every person who has an entry in the main *DNB* from earliest times up to 1950, together with a finding reference to the volume and page number in which the main article is to be found. There is also a recently published *Chronological and Occupational Index to the DNB*.

Among the reliable standard works usually found in most reference libraries, and handy for quick reference, are *Chambers Biographical Dictionary*, A. M. Hyamson's *Dictionary of Universal Biography* (now brought up to date and re-written), and *Webster's Biographical Dictionary*. Haydn's *Universal Index of Biography*, long out of print but often found in secondhand bookshops at a very reasonable price, is a useful source for dates of persons omitted from the modern dictionaries. Some foreign countries publish their own equivalents of the *DNB*; these are listed under 'Biography' in the *Guide to Reference Material*, vol. 2, under each country.

The *Biography Index*, published by H. W. Wilson of New York, claims to be international, but has a definite American bias. More useful is the *Biography and Genealogy Master Index*, produced by Gale Research of Detroit, USA, which, in its microfiche cumulative version, is currently available only at copyright and major libraries in the United Kingdom. Information is extracted from over 600 English language biographical dictionaries, and the 'Bio-Base' (as the microfiche is known) is regularly updated. Birth and death dates are stated, together with the source in abbreviated form, and references to sources can be verified in the accompanying booklet.

In Germany a massive international research tool, the *Index Bio-Bibliographicus Notorum Hominum*, is in preparation which, when completed in a few years' time, will contain both a bibliography and an index to about 2,000 bibliographical works from all countries and in all languages; it is currently being produced in instalments.

Encyclopedias are another source of brief lives; some of the articles are followed by a select bibliography which will lead the researcher on to further source-material. The *McGraw Hill Encyclopedia of World Biography* is excellent. On a national level there is the *Who's Who in History* series, which covers the British Isles from the year 55 BC to 1837, the entries being arranged chronologically according to the date of death. Among other useful works are the three volumes, *Lives of the Tudor Age*, *Lives of the Stuart Age*, and *Lives of the Georgian Age*, each containing approximately 300 lives of a particular period, ranging from a few hundred words to a few thousand per entry; they also include short bibliographies and an indication of the location of major portraits. Feminists may like to know of the *Europa Biographical Dictionary of British Women*, which contains 1,000 entries from Boadicea to the present day; whereas the *Macmillan Dictionary of Women's Biography* includes women of outstanding achievement and influence from all parts of the world.

There are any number of biographical dictionaries relating to the various professions, and the researcher should always ask at the library desk for them. Titles include H. M. Colvin's *Biographical Dictionary of British Architects*; *The New Grove Dictionary of Music and Musicians*; and the two standard works of international biographical reference in the art world, the 10-volume Bénézit, *Dictionnaire des peintres, sculpteurs, dessinateurs et graveurs* and the 37-volume Thieme and Becker, *Allgemeines Lexikon der bildenden Künstler*. For theatrical lives, a major project is under way in the United States: a *Biographical Dictionary of Actors, Actresses, Musicians, Dancers, Managers and Other Stage Personnel in London 1660-1800*; so far, some ten volumes (A-N) have been published. *Munk's Roll* (lives of Fellows of the Royal College of Physicians) contains biographical information on apothecaries and doctors from the 16th century to the present day.

The *Oxford Companion* series are another useful source of biographical information. Volumes include *American History*, *Art*, *Canadian Literature*, *Children's Literature*, *Classical Literature*, the *Decorative Arts*, *English Literature*, *Film*, *French Literature*, *German Literature*, *Law*, *Music*, *Ships and the Sea*, *Spanish Literature* and the *Theatre*.

The best quick reference for contemporary biography is *Who's Who*. There are also seven *Who Was Who* volumes containing entries for those who died during the years 1897-1980, and a *Cumulated Index* volume (1897-1980). Some professions and religious groups have their own biographical volumes, as for example *Crockford's Clerical Directory*, the *Jewish Year Book*, the *Medical Register*, the *Writers' Directory*, and a whole series of *Who's Who* volumes in various fields (*Art*, *Journalism*, *Music*, the *Theatre*, *Government*, *Finance and Industry*, *Yachting*, and many more), some of which are annual and others published at irregular intervals. There are also *Who's Who* volumes for many foreign countries.

Among the more international reference works of contemporary biography are *Who's Who in the World*, the *International Who's Who* and the *Dictionary of International Biography*, all of which include entries on a worldwide basis. Other useful sources are the *International Authors' and Writers' Who's Who*, the *International Year Book and Statesman's Who's Who*, *Who's Who in International Organizations* and *Who's Who in Europe* (this is in French). Foreign biographical sources are listed under selected individual countries (see pages 127-40).

Bibliographies

The best way to find out what has already been published about a person is to consult the general catalogue of one of the major libraries, using whatever 'Recent Acquisitions' or computer-updated listing is available, and also – remembering that new books take some time to reach the library shelf and catalogue – checking recent issues of the *BNB*. In the case of a prominent figure of history or literature, there may already be a published bibliography, and this can be traced in the *World Bibliography of Bibliographies*, usually to be found on the reference shelves of major libraries, and comprehensive up to 1974. Again, this should be supplemented by a search in the general catalogue and/or *BNB* for works published since that date.

Up-to-date bibliographies will be found in the most recently published studies of the subject, and it is a good investment to buy rather than borrow such a book, so that you can keep it at your elbow and make notes and underlinings in it of special sources; alternatively, make a photocopy of the bibliography section. Such bibliographies make an excellent starting point for research; with luck, they will include references to newspaper and periodical articles. Where this is not so, a search should be made in the *British Humanities Index* and the earlier subject indexes to periodicals (see pages 41-2).

Obituaries

Obituaries are an excellent source and often the starting point for biographical research, since the more recent notices usually provide both an outline of a person's life and an evaluation of his career.

To find notices of people who died earlier than the mid-19th century, the 6-volume *Musgrave's Obituary* is the first place to look;

you should also use the *Indexes to the Biographical and Obituary Notices* in the *Gentleman's Magazine* (the two volumes cover the years 1731-1819) and, if you know the approximate year of death, the *Annual Register*. For obituaries of prominent persons who have died since the early 1800s, *The Times* is the best source; in recent years as many as 600 obituary notices have been printed annually in that paper. Provided you have an approximate date of death, a search in the *Times Index* should not take long, while for recent obituary notices there are now three published volumes, *Obituaries from The Times*, for the years 1951-1960, 1961-1970 and 1971-1975.

Not everyone you may expect to find in *The Times* has achieved an obituary there (much depends on how many other eminent people died the same day), and so the *Daily Telegraph*, the *Guardian* and the relevant local newspapers should be checked. The local paper of the area in which a person was resident often prints a notice that did not 'make' the nationals or one that goes into greater detail. Professional and trade journals, where appropriate, are especially useful for the evaluation of a person's career.

International notices, but with an American bias, are best checked in the *New York Times Obituaries Index*, covering 1858 to 1979, and in the *New York Times Biographical Service*; for notices relating to persons of other countries, look also at the relevant national paper.

Diaries, letters and memoirs

A great deal of information will be obtained about a person from the published diaries, letters or memoirs of their friends and contemporaries. As research progresses, therefore, it is an excellent plan to keep an ongoing list of all names that crop up and systematically to check these out at the library. Use the indexes to these books to locate the relevant passages. If you think there may be unpublished journals or correspondence, consult the National Register of Archives, as explained earlier in this chapter under the heading 'Private Papers'.

School and university records

School and university records provide excellent source material, not only for details of a person's scholastic and academic achievement, but also for information concerning his extra-curricular activities (sports, drama, public-speaking, etc.) and — especially important —

the names of his contemporaries and friends, schoolmasters and tutors. Should any of these people still be alive, they may have useful contributions to make and can usually be traced through the school or university, or – if they themselves have achieved eminence – in the current *Who's Who*.

The Institute of Historical Research pamphlet, *Registers of the Universities, Colleges and Schools of Great Britain and Ireland* lists the printed registers that existed at the date of publication (1966); others may be looked up in library catalogues. Where no register exists, the school secretary or secretary of the relevant 'Old Boys' or 'Old Girls' association will often be of great assistance. Research of this kind may involve you in a visit to the educational establishment concerned. Addresses, with names of current headmasters and headmistresses, will be found in the *Public and Preparatory Schools Yearbook*, the *Girls' School Yearbook*, or the *Independent Schools Association Year Book*, or may be obtained from the local education authority. Universities and colleges are listed in the *World of Learning*. The registers of Oxford and Cambridge, *Alumni Oxonienses* and *Alumni Cantabrigienses*, and A. B. Emden's *Biographical Registers* of both these universities to 1500 are of special value to the historian, while the *Historical Registers* series (also for Oxford and Cambridge) bring the records up to the present day.

Service records

You should encounter no great problem in obtaining details of a person's Service career. All records more than 100 years old are at the Public Record Office, where there are also complete runs of the *Army*, *Navy* and *Air Force Lists*; current volumes of these are usually available in all reference libraries.

Regimental histories are another good source and may be traced in the Society for Army Historical Research's *Bibliography of Regimental Histories*. J. M. Brereton's *Guide to the Regiments and Corps of the British Army* includes, along with other information, addresses of regimental headquarters to whom to write for further details; the same author's more recent publication, *The British Soldier: A Social History*, is essential reading for writers needing to know about Army life from the mid-17th century onwards. Another highly recommended book is G. Hamilton-Edwards' *In Search of Army Ancestry*. The Public Record Office leaflet no. 9, 'British Military Records as sources for Biography and Genealogy', is obtainable on request from the PRO, Ruskin Avenue, Kew, Richmond, Surrey TW9 4DU.

So far as naval records are concerned, the National Maritime Museum has published a useful list, *The Commissioned Sea Officers of the Royal Navy 1660-1815*; another informative source-book is the *Dictionary of British Ships and Seamen*. The whereabouts of the records of all three Services can be ascertained from R. Higham's admirable *Guide to the Sources of British Military History*.

Business records

Details of a person's business career can often be obtained from the organization or company by whom he or she was employed. Naturally there are sometimes restrictions on the amount of information that will be divulged to an outsider, but in special circumstances the researcher may be allowed access to the relevant files.

There may be a company history, either published or printed for private circulation, which will provide extremely useful background material. Annual returns and other statutory documents, including lists of all directors and company secretaries, of public, private limited and guarantee companies may be inspected (on microfiche) at Companies House (Department of Trade and Industry), 55 City Road, London EC1Y 1BB (tel. 01-253 9393) or at the Companies Registration Office, Crown Way, Maindy, Cardiff CF4 3UZ (tel. Cardiff (0222) 45915); a modest search fee is payable per file, and there are full photocopying facilities. The Business Archives Council, Denmark House, 15 Tooley Street, London SE1 2PN (tel. 01-407 6110) maintains a library and will advise researchers about records available; its Scottish counterpart, the Business Archives Council of Scotland, is at the University of Glasgow, G12 8QQ (tel. Glasgow (041) 339 8855, ext. 7516). Researchers may also use the British Library Business Information Service, based at the Holborn branch of the Science Reference Library, 25 Southampton Buildings, Chancery Lane, London WC2A 1AW (tel. 01-404 0406).

Members of Parliament and government officials

Dod's Parliamentary Companion, first published in 1832, is the indispensable British biographical source-book for the modern period. Earlier information will be found in the Institute of Historical Research series (9 volumes published to date), *Office Holders in Modern Britain*. There is one volume per ministry, some of the lists beginning in 1660 and covering the entire period up to

1870; the latest volume in the series lists officials of Royal Commissions of Inquiry 1815-70. For the location of private papers of Members of Parliament and selected public servants, consult *Sources in British Political History 1900-1951.*

Bidwell's Guide to Government Ministers 1900-1972 is international in coverage.

Public speeches and broadcasts

Speeches of any significance are usually reported in the national press and may be traced in the *Times Index* either under the speaker's name or under the name of the society or conference addressed. The text of Members' speeches in Parliament are printed in *Hansard: Parliamentary Debates* (separate series for the House of Commons and the House of Lords). Lectures or papers read before learned or professional bodies will normally be found in the transactions or proceedings of such institutions at a later date.

To check on broadcasts since 1979, use the microfiche *BBC Programme Index* if it is available in your local library; otherwise apply to the BBC Written Archives Centre, Caversham Park, Reading, Berks RG4 8TZ (tel. Reading (0734) 472742). The index to *The Listener* is always worth a try if you have access to it, but not all libraries possess a complete run of the periodical, in spite of the fact that it is available on microfilm 1929-84 or on microfiche from 1980 onwards.

Travel

Obtaining information about a person's travel may be unexpectedly complicated, where no diary or travelogue was kept. Hotel registers and shipping company records are not always retained for more than a few years, although it is always worth asking. (For example, the P. & O. Group's archives were deposited at the National Maritime Museum in Greenwich in the autumn of 1977.)

British Transport historical records are now at the Public Record Office in Kew, and so are the records of the former Board of Trade (now the Department of Trade and Industry) of more than 100 years ago; the latter contain lists of all arrivals in, and departures from, the United Kingdom, but only a sample (roughly one-tenth) of passengers' lists and ships' logs, so that it is very much a matter of luck whether the information you seek will be obtainable. For more recent information you should write to the Registrar-General of

Shipping and Seamen, Llantrisant Road, Llandaff, Cardiff CF5 2YS. Factual details such as dates of departure, ports of call, tonnage, and which company owns a particular vessel may be quite easily verified in *Lloyd's Shipping Index*, *Lloyd's Voyage Record* or the *ABC Shipping Guide*.

Further Research

Having cast your net, and hauled in your initial catch of material, your next task as biographer will be to sort the documentation into periods, or other natural chapters, of the life and, as you proceed, to make a note of any supplementary research to be undertaken. For a short biographical feature or the synopsis of a book, you can fairly safely rely on the standard or most recent work, plus your own special knowledge; but if you are embarking on a full-length biography you must go through and evaluate for yourself all the published material. It is a good idea to make index cards or slips for each book or article read, and to keep these in alphabetical sequence; this will take only a few minutes at the time and will be of immense value both for quick reference as you write and at the end of the day, when it comes to compiling the bibliography (see chapter 10, 'Preparation for the Press', page 143).

Some professional help may be required for your chapter on family ancestry (see 'Specialist Research', pages 120-1) and if so, this should be arranged at the earliest possible moment, as good genealogists are frequently booked up for several months ahead. At the same time the question of employing outside researchers should also be carefully considered: where the source material is located at some distance from your home, or if it is essential to go through several years of a particular paper that is available only at the British Newspaper Library at Colindale, for instance, it may pay you to off-load part of the routine research and leave yourself free to tackle the more complicated aspects of the work.

Inevitably some travelling will be involved, and it makes sense to plan this so that several sources and/or interviews can be combined on each trip. A visit to the family home, if it still exists, is essential, and on such a visit time must be allowed for conversations with local inhabitants and – particularly important – with anyone close to the family who is still alive, such as a gardener, nanny or cook, where appropriate, or perhaps the vicar or local schoolmaster or publican. It goes without saying that this applies only when you are researching for biographies of people who are either still alive or recently deceased; in the case of subjects who were born earlier than the turn of the century, you have no choice but to rely on documentary sources such as the local newspaper or church magazine, or the records of any local societies with which the family is known to have been connected. The local librarian or secretary of the local historical society will usually be helpful in this respect, and you could strike lucky in that the descendants of an old family retainer may have cherished stories handed down verbally from one generation to the next, along with old photographs or other mementoes, so that any opportunity of visiting such people should always be taken up.

Corroboration of family births, marriages and deaths since 1837 can be obtained at the General Register Office, and of divorces and Wills from the Principal Registry of the Family Division at Somerset House (for details and how to trace earlier records, see chapter 8 on 'Family and Local History', pages 103-18). To verify the date of an engagement you may need to search the appropriate pages of *The Times*, *Daily Telegraph* or local paper; these papers will also carry reports of christenings, weddings, funerals and memorial services in the case of prominent members of society.

If the subject of your biography was involved in any major legal proceedings, you will be able to check this in the *All England Law Reports*, which begin in 1558 and are indexed; or use the *Times Index* and look up the law report in that paper (these have been published since January 1788). Once you have the date of the court proceedings you can, if you require a more popular account or a 'sensational' headline to quote, then look up other newspapers of the same date.

Special Problems

Names

In private correspondence and diaries people are often mentioned by nickname or Christian name only, and their identity may not be clear to you at the outset of research. It is an excellent idea to keep an alphabetical list or card index of everyone who crops up in the course of your work on a biography; apart from its value to you personally as a private 'who's who' of identification, it will come in very useful should any editorial note be required and also later on for the index. Among pitfalls to avoid are the danger of confusing titles (always check on which duke or earl you are referring to at any one time) and the various names by which a woman may be known during her life, due to a series of marriages and/or divorces and the possibility that she may have reverted to her maiden name for professional or other reasons.

Dating letters

Letters all too frequently present the biographer with unforeseen problems. Far too many people had (and still have) the habit of dating their correspondence 'Thursday', 'Sunday, 12th' or 'Amsterdam, Monday', or – which is worse from the researcher's point of view – of not dating them at all. You should also be aware that some individuals are prone to stuff free hotel or club stationery into their briefcases and to use it weeks or even months later, so that although such correspondence may be dated, you cannot be absolutely certain that the writer was actually resident at the hotel or club at the time: if there is any doubt at all in your mind on this score, try to verify the date and/or place in another source.

Some expert detective work will sometimes be needed before you can establish the correct chronological sequence of a bundle of correspondence. The most obvious clues are: the address from which the letter is, or is alleged to be, written; the person to whom it is written; the subject-matter. Look also at the handwriting; the ink; the paper: should there be a watermark, this will not give you the precise date of the letter, but it will provide firm evidence that the document cannot have been written earlier than the date of the watermark.

If, on first reading, a letter does not appear to offer any clue of this kind, do not despair. Re-examine it closely for mention of any family, national or world event – perhaps the death of a well-known person, an exhibition or play seen, a new novel read, and so on, the dates of which can then be checked out in the national press, *Whitaker's Almanack* and other sources. Letters that you cannot even guess at dating should be kept apart from the rest; sooner or later, as work progresses, you are more than likely to stumble on some information (nearly always when you are not looking for it) that will enable you to slot such letters into their right sequence. The use of the *Handbook of Dates for Students of English History* for checking the day of the week of given dates has been explained on page 62.

Handwriting is a great revealer of character, and biographers are sometimes tempted to send a few letters for analysis by a graphologist. If you decide to do this, ask the Membership Secretary, British Institute of Graphology, Enderby House, Enderby Road, Chester CH1 4AH, for a recommendation, and be sure to send correspondence of varying dates. Among a number of books on the subject, Diane Simpson's *The Analysis of Handwriting* is an excellent guide: in addition to much practical information, it contains an entertaining short chapter on the analysis of 'doodles'.

Verbal information

It is beyond the scope of this chapter to examine in detail all the possibilities open to the biographical researcher, but if the basic principle is followed of taking each natural phase of the life in turn, verifying dates and events in printed and other records and supplementing the documentary material with the recollections of contemporaries wherever obtainable, you will not go far wrong. A word of warning about the use of verbal information, however: human nature being what it is, people do frequently tend to try to enhance their own status (either in the researcher's eyes or their own or with a view to their name appearing in print) by exaggerating their intimacy or acquaintance with a well-known person, and memories in general are, sadly, far from infallible. Always, therefore, make a point of double-checking, so far as you can, any story that is told to you. If you cannot verify it from a reliable printed source, try to get corroboration from a second person. Confidences must, of course, be respected at all times, and care must be taken to avoid giving offence to relatives or other persons who are still alive.

Where private individuals have been especially helpful or informative, it is good manners to let them see the draft text before going to press, and to acknowledge their assistance in the book.

ABC Shipping Guide, published monthly since 1952 by ABC Travel Guides Ltd, Dunstable, Beds.
Air Force List, published annually since 1949 by HMSO, London
All England Law Reports: reprint 1558-1935, 36 vols + index, Butterworth, London, 1966-8; since 1936 weekly, with annual cumulative index, Butterworth, London
Alumni Cantabrigienses: A Biographical List of all known Students, Graduates and Holders of Office to 1900, by J. & J. A. Venn, 10 vols, Cambridge University Press, 1940-54; Kraus reprint, 1974
Alumni Oxonienses: The Members of the University of Oxford 1500-1886, 8 vols, by J. Foster, Parker, Oxford, 1888-92; Kraus reprint, 1968

Analysis of Handwriting, The by Diane Simpson, A & C Black, London, 1985

Annual Register, published since 1758 by Longman, London

Army List, now published bi-annually by HMSO, London (first published 1814; but an earlier series exists from 1754 and may be seen at the PRO, Kew)

BBC Programme Index, 1979 onwards, Chadwyck-Healey Ltd, Cambridge (microfiche)

Bibliography of Regimental Histories, compiled by A. S. White, Society for Army Historical Research with The Army Museums Ogilby Trust London, 1965 (now out of print, but the library of the National Army Museum, Royal Hospital Road, London SW3 4HT (tel. 01-730 0717) maintains a fully up-dated interleaved version)

Bidwell's Guide to Government Ministers 1900-1972, 3 vols, Frank Cass, London, 1973-4

Biographical Dictionary of British Architects 1660-1840, rev. ed., by H. M. Colvin, Murray, London, 1978

Biographical Dictionary of World War I, by H. H. Herwig and N. M. Heyman, Greenwood, London, 1982

Biographical Dictionary of World War II, by C. Tunney, Dent, London, 1972

Biographical Register of the University of Cambridge to 1500, by A. B. Emden, Cambridge University Press, 1963

Biographical Register of the University of Oxford to 1500, 3 vols, by A. B. Emden, Clarendon Press, Oxford, 1957-9; supplement (1501-1540), 1974

Biography and Genealogy Master Index, 8 vols, Gale Research, Detroit, 1980, updated regularly on microfiche

British Archives: A Guide to Archive Resources in the United Kingdom, by Janet Foster and Julia Sheppard, Macmillan, London, 1982; paperback ed., 1984

British Humanities Index, published quarterly since 1963, with annual cumulations, by the Library Association, London

British National Bibliography (BNB), published since 1950; since 1974 weekly, with monthly indexes, quarterly and annual cumulations, by British Library Bibliographic Services Division, London

British Soldier, The: A Social History, by J. M. Brereton, Bodley Head, London, 1986

Chambers Biographical Dictionary, rev. ed., 2 vols, Chambers, Edinburgh, 1984

Commissioned Sea Officers of the Royal Navy 1660-1815, National Maritime Museum, London, 1954

Crockford's Clerical Directory, first issued in 1858; new edition, 1985/6, by Church House Publishing, London, 1985

Dictionary of British Ships and Seamen, by G. Uden and R. Cooper, Allen Lane, London, 1981

Dictionary of International Biography, published annually since 1963, now by International Biographical Centre, Cambridge

Dictionary of National Biography (DNB), to 1900, 22 vols, Oxford University Press, London, 1908-9; 7 later vols, each covering 10 years, for the period 1901-1970, the most recent (1961-70) published 1981; compact edition, 2 vols, 1975 (now out of print); *The Concise DNB, Part 1, Beginnings to 1900*, 2nd ed., 1906; *Part 2, 1901-1970*, 1982; *A Chronological and Occupational Index to the DNB*, 1985

Dictionary of Universal Biography, by A. M. Hyamson, first published by Routledge, London, 1916; re-written, 1976; reprinted Routledge, London and Gale Research, Detroit, 1981

Dod's Parliamentary Companion, published annually since 1832 by Dod's Parliamentary Companion Ltd, Herstmonceux, E. Sussex

Europa Biographical Dictionary of British Women, Europa, London, 1983; paperback ed., 1985

Genleman's Magazine: Index to the Biographical and Obituary Notices, 2 vols, *1731-1780*, British Record Society, London, 1891; *1781-1819*, by B. Nangle, Garland Publishing, New York and London, 1980

Girls' School Yearbook, published annually by A & C Black, London

Grove Dictionary of Music and Musicians, The New, 20 vols, edited by Stanley Sadie, Macmillan, London, 1981

Guide to Reference Material, vol 2, 4th ed., ed. A. J. Walford, Library Association, London, 1982

Guide to the Papers of British Cabinet Ministers 1900-1951, compiled by C. Hazelhurst and C. Woodland, Royal Historical Society, London, 1974

Guide to the Regiments and Corps of the British Army, by J. M. Brereton, Bodley Head, London, 1985

Guide to the Sources of British Military History, ed. R. Higham, Routledge, London, 1972

Handbook of Dates for Students of English History, ed C. R. Cheney, Royal Historical Society, London, 1945; latest reprint, 1982

Hansard's Parliamentary Debates: House of Commons and *House of Lords*, published as official reports since 1909 by HMSO, London; earlier series of *House of Commons Debates* published by Hansard, London, from 1806

Haydn's Universal Index of Biography, ed. J. Bertrand Payne, Moxon, London, 1870

Historical Register series (Universities of Cambridge and Oxford):
   Cambridge, to year 1910, with supplementary vols, Cambridge University Press; latest vol (1971-5), 1977
   Oxford, 1220-1900, with supplementary vols to 1965, Oxford University Press, 1900, 1970

Independent Schools Association Year Book, published annually by the Independent Schools Association, Cambridge

Index Bio-Bibliographicus Notorum Hominum, Biblio Verlag, Osnabrück, in progress, 1972-

In Search of Army Ancestry, by G. Hamilton-Edwards, Phillimore, Chichester, 1977

International Authors' and Writers' Who's Who, 10th ed., International Biographical Centre, Cambridge, 1986

International Who's Who, published annually by Europa Publications, London

International Year Book and Statesman's Who's Who, previously published by Burke's Peerage, London, now by Thomas Skinner Directories, East Grinstead, W. Sussex

Jewish Year Book, published annually by Jewish Chronicle Publications, London

Listener, The, published weekly since 1929 by BBC Publications, London

Lives of the Georgian Age, Lives of the Stuart Age, Lives of the Tudor Age, 3 vols, Osprey, London, 1976-8

Lloyd's Shipping Index, first published 1880, now daily by Lloyd's of London Press Ltd, Colchester, Essex

Lloyd's Voyage Record, published weekly since 1946 by Lloyd's of London Press Ltd, Colchester, Essex

McGraw Hill Encyclopedia of World Biography, 12 vols, McGraw Hill, New York and London, 1973

Macmillan Dictionary of Women's Biography, ed. J. S. Uglow, Macmillan, London, 1982; paperback ed., 1984

Medical Register, published annually by the General Medical Council, London

Munk's Roll (Lives of the Fellows of the Royal College of Physicians), 7 vols published to date, covering 16th century to 1983, IRL Press, Oxford, continuing

Musgrave's Obituary prior to 1800, 6 vols, ed. Sir G. J. Armytage, Harleian Society, London, 1899-1901

Navy List, published annually since 1814 by HMSO, London (earlier listings at PRO, Kew)

New York Times Biographical Service, published monthly since 1970

New York Times Obituaries Index, 1858-1968, New York, 1970; *1969-79*, Glen Rock, N.J., 1980

Obituaries from The Times, 3 vols covering the period 1951-75, Research Publications, Reading, 1975-9

Office Holders in Modern Britain, 9 vols, Institute of Historical Research, London, 1972-84

Oxford Companion series, Oxford University Press, regularly revised; some paperback editions

Public and Preparatory Schools Yearbook, published annually by A & C Black, London

Registers of the Universities, Colleges and Schools of Great Britain and Ireland, by P. M. Jacobs, Institute of Historical Research, London, 1964 (reprinted from the Institute's *Bulletin*, 37 (November 1964))

Sources in British Political History, 1900-1951, edited by Chris Cook, Macmillan, London: 1 *A Guide to the Archives of Selected Organisations and Societies*, 1975; 2 *A Guide to the Papers of Selected Public Servants*, 1975; 3 *A Guide to the Private Papers of Members of Parliament, A-K*, 1977; 4 *A Guide to the Private Papers of Members of Parliament, L-Z*, 1977; 5 *A Guide to the Private Papers of Selected Writers, Intellectual Publicists*, 1978; 6 *First Consolidated Supplement*, 1984

Statesman's Year Book, The, published annually since 1864 by Macmillan, London

The Times Index, first published 1790; now monthly, with annual cumulations, Research Publications, Reading

Webster's Biographical Dictionary, Merriam, Springfield, Mass., latest edition, 1980

Whitaker's Almanack, published annually by J. Whitaker, London

Who Was Who, published by A & C Black, London; 7 vols to date, covering the period 1897-1980; *Cumulated Index 1897-1980*, 1981

Who's Who in History series, 5 vols, Blackwell, Oxford, 1966-75, now out of print

World Bibliography of Bibliographies, 4th ed., by T. Besterman, Societas Bibliographica, Lausanne, 1965-6; supplement, covering the period 1964-74, by A. F. Toomey, Rowman and Littlefield, Totowa, N.J., 1977

World of Learning, The, 2 vols, published biennially by Europa Publications, London

Writers Directory, The, St James Press, London/St Martin's Press, New York, latest ed., 1986

Note: Space does not permit a complete listing of *Who's Who* volumes for the various professions and foreign countries, of which there are now some 70 titles published by a number of different firms; however, the researcher should have no difficulty in tracing these in the major library catalogues.

7

Family and Local History

In recent years people have become increasingly interested in tracing their own family ancestry, and, largely as a result of teaching in schools and evening classes, many students embark on a local or family history project which they later wish to develop into a full-length study. Biographers and authors of historical novels also need to do some research in this field, and some of the problems they are likely to encounter have been outlined in the sections of this handbook on 'Historical and factual research' and 'Biography'.

The first thing to be said is that research for family or local history can be exceedingly complex. For those who look on it as a hobby and for whom time is no object, it will be a lengthy and often frustrating, but always in the end rewarding, task. Writers with publishers' press deadlines to meet, and who need only certain facts to fill out their work – for example, ancestral research for the first chapter of a biography, or the tracing of a particular Will, or the detail of some event in a certain parish needed for an historical novel – would be well advised to use the services of a professional genealogist or record agent (see 'Specialist Research', pages 120-1). Those who wish to undertake their own research in this field should be prepared to do a considerable amount of preliminary study so as to familiarize themselves with the classes of records available and the kind of information to be derived from them.

Space does not permit to do more here than suggest the major sources of information, as well as some of the standard textbooks on genealogy and local archives. Most adult education centres run courses on local history and genealogy, but very few on palaeography (the study of old handwriting). A comprehensive course, leading to a diploma, may be followed, on a full- or part-time basis, or as a correspondence course, at the Institute of Heraldic and Genealogical Studies, 79-82 Northgate, Canterbury, Kent CT1 1BA (tel. Canterbury (0227) 68664). The Institute's well-stocked library is open to non-members on Mondays, Wednesdays and Fridays, for a fee of £3.00 per half-day or £5.00 per day, by appointment with the librarian.

The Society of Genealogists, 14 Charterhouse Buildings, Goswell Road, London EC1M 7BA (tel. 01-251 8799) periodically organizes day conferences and lectures for beginners (members only). Members of the Society have free use of the library, with its unique collection of printed, manuscript and microfilmed material, free attendance at lectures and the benefit of a reduced rate for research carried out by members of the staff; they also receive a quarterly journal, *Genealogists' Magazine*. The writer who intends to do any extensive genealogical research, and who lives in or with good access to London, will find membership of the Society very worthwhile. Non-members may use the library on payment of a small fee, currently £2.00 for one hour, £5.00 for 3½ hours, £7.50 for a whole day.

There are family history societies and local history groups in most counties of the United Kingdom, and writers researching in this field should consider joining their local group. Subscriptions are usually quite modest, and in return members benefit from advice on their researches as well as the exchange of information with fellow genealogists and historians. An up-to-date list of these societies, giving the secretaries' names and addresses, is available on receipt of a stamped addressed envelope plus 26p in stamps, from the Administrator, Federation of Family History Societies (FFHS), 31 Seven Star Road, Solihull, West Midlands B91 2BZ.

Among a number of journals of interest are *Family History News and Digest*, published twice a year (spring and autumn) by the FFHS; *Family History*, the quarterly journal of the Institute of Heraldic and Genealogical Studies; and *The Local Historian* (formerly *The Amateur Historian*), now published by the British Association for Local History (BALH), The Mill Manager's House, Cromford Mill, Matlock, Derbyshire DE4 3RQ. There is also a most useful series of booklet guides on various aspects of genealogical research published by the FFHS (list on application). Finally, a subscription to the annual *Genealogical Research Directory* (currently £9.75 in the UK) entitles you to register up to 15 names in which you are interested; the book is circulated throughout the world and may well bring you the bonus of an exchange of information with other subscribers.

Using County Record Offices, Archaeological Societies and Other Collections

The writer embarking on a family or local history should first of all make a visit to his local record office, where the archivist or an assistant archivist will usually be glad to discuss the project and to explain what records are available. Some county record offices publish useful pamphlets for students on how to trace the history of a parish or of a family, and most have a printed or mirofiche guide to their collections, as well as regularly updated lists of parish registers and other documents that have been deposited.

A short list of record offices will be found in Appendix 1, but more detailed information is given in the HMSO pamphlet, *Record Repositories in Great Britain*, which is revised every few years. A few record offices changed their names on 1 April 1974, when the new county boundaries came into force: a fully up-to-date list of counties will be found in the current *Whitaker's Almanack* or the *Municipal Year Book*.

The principal public libraries have local history collections, and those of local archaeological societies are usually open to *bona fide* researchers (non-members may be asked to pay a modest search fee). Where information is needed from outside your own district, it is always worth sending a preliminary letter (with self-addressed stamped envelope) to the local archivist or chief reference librarian. Most county archivists are happy to answer simple enquiries, such as the verification of not more than one or two entries in a parish register (a baptism, marriage or burial), but especially nowadays, due to the severe cutback in local government expenditure, staff are not available to undertake extensive searches. However, advice will always be given on the records to consult, as well as practical help over any problems encountered in the search room; and most county record offices will, on request, also supply the names and addresses of local record agents. Photocopies and photographs of most documents are usually obtainable.

A list of local archaeological societies, with names and addresses of secretaries, will be found in *Whitaker's Almanack*.

Family History

A family history may have as its starting point a rough tree drawn up by a relative or ancestor, or – if you are lucky – a more professional pedigree and possibly also a collection of papers handed down from one generation to another or recently discovered in an attic of the ancestral home. The first thing to do is to make reasonably sure that a history has not already been written. This can be checked in one of several ways: in the catalogue or subject index of one of the copyright libraries; at the library of the Society of Genealogists; at the local record office nearest to the family home. Remember that many family histories are privately printed or may be deposited at the record office, or donated to the local library, in typescript.

If the family is likely to have been recorded in any of Burke's publications, the place to look is *Burke's Family Index*. This useful volume has references to some 20,000 different family histories.

The next step is to verify, one by one, the dates of all births, marriages and deaths, and – other people's memories being what they are – also to check the names, allowing for variations in spelling. The usual procedure is to work methodically backwards in time, either from yourself or from the person you are writing about, first to the parents, then the grandparents, and so on, generation by generation. It is a good idea to make a card index, with a separate card for each individual, on which data is entered as it is verified; the researcher can design his own system, or there are specially printed genealogical record cards or 'research workbooks' on the market (available from the Society of Genealogists, among others).

You can draw up your own draft family tree as you proceed; but if the tree is to be published, it is best to have it professionally drawn.

Verifying births, marriages and deaths

Since 1 July 1837 all births, marriages and deaths in England and Wales, together with some overseas (consular) and service returns, births and deaths at sea, etc. have been centrally recorded at the General Register Office in London. Formerly at Somerset House, these records are now permanently at St Catherine's House, 10 Kingsway, London WC2B 6JP. In Scotland registration began in 1855, the records being housed at the office of the Registrar General, New Register House, Edinburgh EH1 3YT. In Ireland, the records from 1864 to 1921 are at the office of the Registrar General, Custom House, Dublin, for the whole of the country and for the Republic since 1922; Northern Ireland records dating from partition are in the care of the Registrar General, Oxford House, 49-55 Chichester Street, Belfast BT1 4HL.

Searches may be made in person at St Catherine's House but access is only to the indexes, not to the actual registers. The index volumes are arranged according to the quarter of the year in which the event (birth, marriage or death) was registered, and alphabetically under surnames. Unless you have an approximate date to go on, you must be prepared for a long haul – and an exhausting one, as pulling out one heavy volume after another is exceedingly tiring. The information printed in the indexes is minimal, so that sometimes you may not be certain that you have found the correct entry; but if you request a copy of the relevant certificate and the parentage and/or spouse does not match with the information you have to give on the application form, a refund will be made. As full certificates now cost £5.00 apiece, this is an important consideration. (There is a shorter form of certificate – available for births only – costing £2.50, but this is not normally sufficient for genealogical research purposes as it contains only the name, sex, date and place, but *not* the parentage.)

It is always worth getting copies of birth, marriage and death certificates, as the detail given on them, such as the occupation of a child's father, the witnesses to a marriage, the cause of death and the address at which it occurred, will be invaluable and may also lead to other channels of enquiry. For those who live a long way from London (or Edinburgh, Dublin or Belfast), copies of certificates may be obtained by post, in which case a higher fee is charged (currently £10.00 for a full certificate, £7.50 for a short birth certificate); this normally includes a search over a period of five years, but there are slight variations between the different registries.

More than 80 million birth and baptismal entries, and some marriage entries, may be seen on the International Genealogical Index (IGI), formerly known as the Computer File Index, of the Genealogical Society of the Church of Jesus Christ of Latter-Day Saints, Salt Lake City, Utah, USA (known more familiarly as the Mormon Church), which is available on microfiche in the UK. The complete world listing of the IGI may be seen in London at the Mormon Branch Library (its official title is the London Regional Genealogical Library), 64-68 Exhibition Road, South Kensington, London SW7 2PA (tel. 01-589 8561) and at the Society of Genealogists; most county record offices and some public libraries hold smaller sections relevant to their own areas. An updated, revised version of the 1984 IGI will be available in the UK from early 1986. The Index is a useful starting point for family history research, as within each county the entries are arranged in alphabetical order of surname. You can obtain on-the-spot print-outs for study at home; in addition, microfilms with fuller information will be sent from Salt Lake City (you pay only for postage). Time-saving as this great research tool is, users of the IGI should, however, be aware that it is neither comprehensive nor, sadly, 100% accurate: coverage and the degree of accuracy vary from county to county (a computer index is, after all, only as accurate as the information fed into it by the human computer operator), so that researchers must always double-check entries in the original sources. (For further details see the FFHS booklet, *Where to Find the International Genealogical Index*.) Also at this Library are the Parish and Vital Records Listings (a guide to parishes, towns and other centres worldwide whose records have been transcribed and/or indexed); an index to the Genealogical Library Catalogue (microfilms obtainable from Salt Lake City); and the Family Registry List (names and addresses of people doing genealogical research and the names which they are researching).

Nonconformist registers were required by law to be surrendered to the Registrar General in 1840, and these are now at the Public Record Office. (Some registers were exempt – where they were kept in the same books as other records, such as members' lists, minutes of meetings, etc. – and you may be lucky enough to find them at local record offices.) The Society of Friends, before surrendering their records, prepared 'Digest Registers' which, together with other valuable Quaker material, may be seen at Friends' House, Euston Road, London NW1 2BJ (tel. 01-387 3601). Records of Huguenots in England since the mid-16th century have been published by the Huguenot Society, University College, Gower Street, London WC1E 6BT. For further information on the existence and whereabouts of Nonconformist registers, see *Sources for Nonconformist Genealogy and Family History* (volume 2 of the *National Index of Parish Registers*).

Researchers seeking material on Roman Catholic or Jewish families should look at volume 3 of the same series, *Sources for Roman Catholic and Jewish Genealogy and Family History*.

Parish registers

Ministers in England were first ordered to keep records of all baptisms, marriages and burials in 1538; some registers therefore start in that year, but others were not commenced until a few years later or the earliest volumes have not survived. Not all parish registers have been deposited at the relevant local record office, but recent legislation provides that clergy who do not have adequate facilities for preservation and storage must deposit them within a reasonable time.

The best way to find out whether a particular parish register has been deposited or not is to telephone to the local record office; with new registers being deposited all the time, the situation is constantly changing. If the record office does not have what you require – and often they will not have registers of recent date – they will give you the name and telephone number of the incumbent in whose possession the relevant registers are, or you can look this up in the current *Crockford's Clerical Directory*. To obtain access to these registers, you must write or telephone to make an appointment, as either the minister or his parish clerk must be present. A fee is payable to the incumbent for this service: at the time of writing he is entitled to ask for £3.00 for up to one hour and £2.00 for each additional hour or part of an hour, but where a longer search is involved it is usually possible to negotiate a more economic fee. Remember that this fee is for searches you make yourself; if you ask the incumbent to make the search for you, he is entitled to charge more for his time.

It is important for the novice researcher to remember that parish registers do not give the exact dates of birth or death, but only those of baptism and burial. (Some of the more diligent parish priests also noted the dates of births and deaths, but not often.) In some parishes there are separate registers for baptisms, marriages and burials; in others, the baptisms and burials may be recorded in the same book, starting at different ends, and where the incumbent ran out of space the entries are sometimes continued a few pages later or, worse, may be merged – you should be careful not to overlook these.

Many registers have been transcribed and/or printed, and the Society of Genealogists issues two very useful booklets: *Parish Register Copies, Part One, Society of Genealogists Collection; Part Two, Other than the Society of Genealogists Collection*. A comprehensive *National Index of Parish Registers*, started a few years ago, is now well under way: the first three volumes constitute a guide to the pre-1837 registers of all denominations in England, Scotland and Wales; in addition, five regional volumes have been published so far, and one on sources for Scottish genealogy and family history. *The Phillimore Atlas and Index of Parish Registers* is another useful research tool (for England and Wales only); or the individual county maps are available from the Institute of Heraldic and Genealogical Studies.

Other useful sources, especially when it is difficult to gain access to the registers, are Bishop's Transcripts (copies of parish registers made by each minister and sent annually to the Bishop of his diocese). Unfortunately these are not altogether reliable, as entries were often copied wrongly, or even omitted, so that it is essential to make a double-check in the original registers.

Marriage indexes

Boyd's Marriage Index, compiled by Mr Percival Boyd from parish registers, Bishop's Transcripts and the marriage licences of England, covers most of the English counties in the period 1538-1837. It contains more than 3½ million names and is housed at the Society of

Genealogists in London; a booklet is available from the Society listing the parishes and dates included. This is an important source for the researcher who already knows the place or county of the marriage he wishes to trace. However, it is neither complete nor infallible (Mr Boyd died in 1955), and entries should always be verified in the relevant parish register. This is a golden rule in genealogical research when using any printed or transcribed registers or indexes.

Another important marriage index is *Pallot's*, containing some 4½ million marriages between 1780 and 1837; this is at the Institute of Heraldic and Genealogical Studies in Canterbury. Enquiries may be sent by post, and searches will be made, subject to a small fee.

There are also a number of local marriage indexes compiled both by family history groups and by individuals, and more are in progress. Ask at your local record office, or consult the FFHS booklet, *Marriage, Census and Other Indexes for Family Historians*.

Marriage registers generally are separate from those of baptisms and burials; some are more informative than others. Supplementary information may be obtained from records of the intention to marry, such as banns, licences, marriage bonds and allegations. Advice on the availability of these will be given by staff on duty in the record office.

Divorce records

The Divorce Registry at Somerset House, Strand, London WC2R 1LP, holds records of all divorces since 1852 and will supply photocopies of decrees. These are useful to the researcher, as they give the date and place of the marriage.

Wills and administrations

Probate records constitute one of the most useful sources of genealogical information. Since 11 January 1858 copies of all wills and administrations in England and Wales have been centralised at the Principal Registry of the Family Division at Somerset House (address as above); they are calendared alphabetically under surnames in the year in which probate was granted (which may be the same as the year of death, but sometimes later). The calendar volumes are on open shelves, and once you have traced the Will or administration you need, the volume containing it will be produced on demand. Brief notes may be made, or alternatively a photocopy ordered.

Prior to 1858 Wills and administrations were proved by the courts which had general jurisdiction, of which the most important were the Prerogative Court of Canterbury (PCC) and the Prerogative Court of York (PCY). The PCC wills are at the Public Record Office in Chancery Lane, London (*not* at Kew), and those of the PCY at the Borthwick Institute, York. Ask at your local record office for details of other courts.

The British Record Society's *Index Library* lists the Wills held at the PRO and at many local record offices, but as a general guide the researcher should first consult J. S. W. Gibson's *Wills and Where to Find Them*, which discusses the availability of probate records in each English county and also explains the jurisdiction of the different courts, as well as the systems operating in Scotland, Ireland, the Channel Islands and the Isle of Man. *An Index to the Wills proved in the Prerogative County of Canterbury 1750-1800* is in progress under the supervision of Anthony J. Camp, Director of Research of the Society of Genealogists. The latter's *Wills and Their Whereabouts* is another standard guide.

Census returns

The 19th-century census returns are a valuable source for the family historian and may be seen on microfilm in the Census Room of the Public Record Office, Portugal Street, London, five minutes' walk from the Chancery Lane building. Returns exist from 1801, but individual names were not recorded until 1841. The most recent return available for public inspection is that of 1881.

The great value of the census to the genealogist is that he will usually find the whole family (or at least those living under the same roof at the appropriate date) recorded together. The returns of 1851 onwards are the most informative, since they give exact ages and places of birth, and also each person's marital status and relationship to the household, whereas the 1841 census return states only their occupations, in what area of the country they were born and, for those over 15 years, ages to the lowest term of five.

It is of course essential to know, if not the exact address at which the family is believed to have been living at the date of the census, at least the parish. The relevant dates are:

> 6 June 1841
> 30 March 1851
> 7 April 1861
> 2 April 1871
> 3 April 1881

Index books are on open shelves in the Census Room, in which you can look up the number of the book and the enumerator's district; this helps you to locate the precise place on the spool. There are pitfalls in that streets may appear half in one enumerator's district and half in another, and not all enumerators, especially in the earlier returns, were scrupulously accurate. It is a little complicated at first, but the PRO staff will assist anyone in difficulties over tracing the right entry or in deciphering the handwriting, which is often far from clear. As delving into census returns nearly always takes longer than one imagines it will, the wise researcher allows plenty of time for it. A useful pamphlet on the subject is John Boreham's *The Census and How to Use It*.

Other records

The above-mentioned are but a few of the sources open to the genealogist/family historian. Searching these will enable you to draw up at least a skeleton family tree as a basis from which to work. The next stage will be to explore the various other classes of records likely to yield further information. Elucidation of the mysteries of Court rolls, Quarter Sessions records, tax returns, Service records, and so on, is best left to the expert, and among excellent textbooks the following are highly recommended: *Genealogy for Beginners* by A. J. Willis and M. Tatchell; *In Search of Ancestry* by G. Hamilton-Edwards; *A Genealogist's Bibliography* by C. R. Humphery-Smith; the 3-volume standard work by F. Smith and D. E. Gardner, *Genealogical Research in England and Wales*; *The Family History Book* by Stella Colwell; and *Tracing Your Ancestors in the Public Record Office* by Jane Cox and Timothy Padfield. The *Family History Annual* (first edition scheduled for publication in autumn 1985) will contain articles by experts on a wide range of genealogical studies and research methods, while *The Family Historian's Enquire Within* by F. C. Markwell and Pauline Saul is a mine of information and reference to be kept at the researcher's elbow. Terrick FitzHugh's recently published *Dictionary of Genealogy* will be invaluable both to the professional and to the amateur researcher: it has over a thousand entries, and includes descriptions and locations of records by county, as well as explanations of obsolete terms and translations of those Latin phrases most likely to be encountered in ancestry research.

Use should also be made of the indexes to proceedings of local archaeological societies and to publications of local family history societies (see pages 104-5). Most public libraries and county record offices possess complete sets of those relating to their districts.

The major printed biographical sources have been discussed under 'Biography' (pages 83-102), but special mention should be made here of the publications issued by Burke's Peerage Ltd. The delayed new edition of *Burke's Peerage and Baronetage* is due to be published in 1987; revised and corrected, and much more comprehensive than any of the previous editions, its most valuable innovation to the researcher will be the cross-reference section to all names. Other titles include *Burke's Dormant and Extinct Peerages*, the 3-volume *Burke's Landed Gentry*, *Burke's Royal Families of the World*, and *Burke's Irish Family Records*.

There is also a new *Debrett's Peerage and Baronetage*, while the older, but more comprehensive, *Cockayne's Complete Peerage*, covering extant, extinct and dormant titles to 1938, and out of print for many years, has recently been reprinted, as has *Cockayne's Complete Baronetage*. *Boutell's Heraldry* and A. C. Fox-Davies' *A Complete Guide to Heraldry* are standard works, while for the amateur there is a useful booklet published for the Standing Conference for Local History, entitled *How to read a Coat of Arms*. The best place to look up a coat of arms when you come across one and do not know to which family it belongs is Papworth's *Ordinary of British Armorials*. Finally, F. L. Leeson's recent *Directory of British Peerages*, which covers earliest times to the present day in one continuous alphabetical listing of titles and surnames, is an invaluable finding aid.

Local History

Local history writing may range from a short article in the local newspaper or county magazine to a full-length academic study. In all cases painstaking research and a good deal of detective work will be necessary; care must be taken to transcribe original documents accurately and to keep a note of all sources. References should normally be quoted in all but the shortest and most 'popular' articles.

There is a vast store of printed and manuscript material open to the local historian, much of it as yet untapped. Some of these sources have been discussed already under Chapter 3 'Basic Sources of Information' (pages 29-56). As with family history, before embarking on a project it is wise to check with the local record office whether the same ground has been covered by someone else; even if nothing has yet been published or deposited, archivists notoriously have their 'ears to the ground' and will usually be aware of any other writers, researchers or students working on parallel lines. A preliminary study of a work of similar nature, even if it deals with a totally different district, can be of considerable help to a writer wondering how to tackle the particular subject he has in mind.

Difficulty may be encountered in reading early documents, and unless you have some knowledge of palaeography and Latin, you may need to use the services of an expert. F. G. Emmison's booklet, *How to Read Local Archives 1550-1700*, will aid the beginner; but if you are seriously interested in learning more about handwriting, you should read L. C. Hector's *The Handwriting of English Documents* and Hilda Grieve's *Examples of English Handwriting 1150-1750*. Lionel Munby's *Secretary Hand: A Beginner's Introduction* is another useful aid for the novice.

The Latin of local records differs considerably from school Latin, and Eileen A. Gooder's *Latin for Local History* is an excellent textbook. C. T. Martin's *The Record Interpreter*, with its invaluable list of Latin abbreviations and glossary of Latin words used in English historical manuscripts and records, first published in 1892 and out of print for many years, became available again in a facsimile edition a few years ago; and another useful reference work is the revised edition of Baxter and Johnson's *Medieval Latin Word List*.

C. R. Cheney's *Handbook of Dates for Students of English History* and Powicke and Fryde's *Handbook of British Chronology* are indispensable aids to dating: they contain not only lists of rulers (with regnal years), Popes, archbishops and other officers of state, but also include saints' days and tables that enable you to work out the day of the week of any date from AD 500 to the year 2000.

All the above-mentioned standard works should be found on the open shelves in county record offices and good reference libraries.

As general introductions to the subject, the researcher should read D. Iredale's *Local History Research and Writing*; also two titles by F. G. Emmison: *Archives and Local History* and *Introduction to Archives*. Books recommended for further reading include W. G. Hoskin's *Local History in England* and *Fieldwork in Local History*, and W. E. Tate's classic, *The Parish Chest*. A. T. Hale's *Local History Handlist* contains useful short bibliographies on a variety of subjects; now out of print, it is worth asking for at the library. An older guide, but still valuable, is the Library Association's *Sources of Local History*. The *Victoria County Histories* (a varying number of volumes per county and still in progress) are standard works. John Richardson's *The Local Historian's Encyclopedia* is a handy paperback for reference purposes.

Depositing papers

Every writer of family or local history, whether or not his work achieves publication, should consider depositing a copy of it, together with any original papers that may have come into his possession, and possibly also his research notes, at the appropriate local record office or, in the case of a family history, at the Society of Genealogists in London. By so doing he will be making a valuable contribution to the store of material on English social history and genealogy for the use of future generations of students and researchers.

Archives and Local History, 2nd ed., by F. G. Emmison, Phillimore, Chichester, 1978

Boutell's Heraldry, rev. ed. by J. P. Brooke-Little, Warne, London, 1983

Burke's Dormant and Extinct Peerages, reprinted 1979

Burke's Family Index, 1976

Burke's Irish Family Records, 1976

Burke's Landed Gentry, 3 vols, 1965-72

Burke's Peerage and Baronetage, 106th ed., 1987

Burke's Royal Families of the World, 2 vols, 1977, 1980

Census and How to Use It, The, by John Boreham, Solihull: obtainable from the FFHS, price 65p post free (UK)

Complete Baronetage (G. E. Cockayne), reprinted in 6 vols, Alan Sutton, Gloucester, 1982

Complete Guide to Heraldry, A, by A. C. Fox-Davies, rev. by J. P. Brooke-Little, Orbis, London, 1985

Complete Peerage of England, Scotland, Ireland, Great Britain and the United Kingdom, Extant, Extinct or Dormant (G. E. Cockayne), 13 vols, London, 1910-59; reprinted in 6 vols, Alan Sutton, Gloucester, 1982

Crockford's Clerical Directory, published since 1858, now owned jointly by the Church Commissioners for England and the Central Board of Finance of the Church of England due to be published every two years; 89th ed. (1985/6), Church House Publishing, London, 1985

Debrett's Peerage and Baronetage, new edition, Debrett's Peerage Ltd and Macmillan, London, 1985

Dictionary of Genealogy, The: A Guide to British Ancestry Research, by Terrick FitzHugh, Alphabooks, Sherborne, Dorset, 1985

Directory of British Peerages, A, by F. L. Leeson, Society of Genealogists, London, 1985

Family Historian's Enquire Within, The, by F. C. Markwell and P. Saul, FFHS, Solihull, 1985

Family History, published quarterly by the Institute of Heraldic and
Genealogical Studies, Canterbury
Family History Annual, ed. M. J. Burchall, first issue autumn 1985,
obtainable from publisher at 3/33 Sussex Square, Brighton,
E. Sussex BN2 5AB
Family History Book, The, by S. Colwell, Phaidon, Oxford, 1980
Family History News and Digest, published twice a year (spring and
autumn) by the Federation of Family History Societies, Solihull
Fieldwork in Local History, 2nd ed., by W. G. Hoskins, Faber,
London, 1982
Genealogical Research Directory, annually since 1982 (UK agent:
Mrs E. Simpson, 2 Stella Grove, Tollerton, Notts NG12 4EY)
Genealogical Research in England and Wales, 3 vols, by F. Smith
and D. E. Gardner, Bookcraft, Salt Lake City, Utah, USA, 1956-64
Genealogist's Bibliography, A, by C. R. Humphery-Smith, Philli-
more, Chichester, 1984
Genealogists' Magazine, published quarterly by the Society of
Genealogists, London
Handbook of British Chronology, 2nd ed., ed. by F. M. Powicke and
E. B. Fryde, Royal Historical Society, London; revised edition in
preparation
Handbook of Dates for Students of English History, by C. R.
Cheney, London, 1945; latest reprint, 1982
Handwriting of English Documents, The, by L. C. Hector, E.
Arnold, London, 1958; now in facsimile reprint, Kohler &
Coombes, Dorking, 1980
How to Read a Coat of Arms, by P. G. Summers, published for the
Standing Conference for Local History by the National Council of
Social Service, London, 1979
How to Read Local Archives 1550-1700, by F. G. Emmison,
Historical Association, London, 1978
Index Library, published for the British Record Society by Philli-
more, Chichester; continuing
*Index to the Wills proved in the Prerogative Court of Canterbury
1750-1800, An*, ed. A. J. Camp, Society of Genealogists, London,
in progress (3 vols to date)
In Search of Ancestry, 4th ed., by G. Hamilton-Edwards, Phillimore,
Chichester, 1983
Introduction to Archives, by F. G. Emmison, Phillimore, Chichester,
1978
Latin for Local History, 2nd ed., by Eileen A. Gooder, Longman,
London, 1978

List of Parishes in Boyd's Marriage Index, A, by R. W. Massey,
  Phillimore, Chichester, for the Society of Genealogists, London,
  1974
Local Historian, The, published quarterly by the British Association
  for Local History, Matlock, Derbyshire
Local Historian's Encyclopedia, The, by John Richardson, Historic-
  al Publications, New Barnet, 1974; reprinted 1985
Local History in England, 3rd ed., by W. G. Hoskins, Longman,
  Harlow, 1984
Local History Research and Writing, by D. Iredale, Phillimore,
  Chichester, 1980
Marriage, Census and Other Indexes for Family Historians, by J. S.
  W. Gibson, obtainable from the FFHS, Solihull, price £1.20 post
  free (UK)
Medieval Latin Word List, by J. H. Baxter and C. Johnson, rev. ed.
  by R. E. Latham, Oxford University Press, Oxford, 1965
Municipal Year Book, published annually by Municipal Publica-
  tions Ltd, London
National Index of Parish Registers, Phillimore, Chichester, for the
  Society of Genealogists, London, in progress (4 introductory vols
  and 5 regional vols to date):
1 *Sources for Births, Marriages and Deaths before 1837*, by D. J.
  Steel, reprinted 1976
2 *Sources for Nonconformist Genealogy and Family History*, by
  D. J. Steel, 1973
3 *Sources for Roman Catholic and Jewish Genealogy and Family
  History*, by D. J. Steel and Edgar R. Samuel, 1974
4 *South East England: Kent, Surrey and Sussex*, 1980
5 *South Midlands and Welsh Border: Gloucestershire,
  Herefordshire, Oxfordshire, Shropshire, Warwickshire and
  Worcestershire*, 3rd ed. revised, 1976
6 Part 1: *The North Midlands: Staffordshire*, 1982
7 *East Anglia: Cambridgeshire, Norfolk and Suffolk*, 1983
11 Part 1: *Durham and Northumberland*, 2nd ed., 1984
12 *Sources for Scottish Genealogy and Family History*, by D. J.
  Steel, 1970
Ordinary of British Armorials (A. W. W. Papworth), 1874; facsimile
  ed. Tabard Publications, London, 1961
Parish Chest, The, 3rd ed., by W. E. Tate, Phillimore, Chichester,
  1983
Parish Register Copies, in two parts, Phillimore, Chichester, for the
  Society of Genealogists, London, updated regularly: 1 *Society of
  Genealogists Collection*, 7th ed., 1985; 2 *Other Collections*, 1978

Phillimore Atlas and Index of Parish Registers, ed. C. Humphery-Smith, Phillimore, Chichester, 1984

Record Interpreter, The, by Charles Trice Martin, 1892; facsimile of 2nd ed. (1910), Kohler & Coombes, Dorking, 1976

Record Repositories in Great Britain, HMSO, London, updated every few years; new edition due 1987

Secretary Hand: A Beginner's Introduction, by Lionel Munby, 1984; available from BALH, The Mill Manager's House, Cromford Mill, Matlock, Derbyshire DE4 3RQ, price £1.00 post free (UK)

Sources of Local History, 4th ed., Library Association, London, 1971

Tracing your Ancestors in the Public Record Office, rev. ed., by Jane Cox and Timothy Padfield, HMSO, London, 1985

Victoria History of the Counties of England series, started in 1899 and still in progress (first volume published 1901), Oxford University Press for the Institute of Historical Research, London

Where to Find the International Genealogical Index, ed. by J. Gibson and M. Walcot, FFHS, Solihull, 1985; available from FFHS price £1.20 post free (UK)

Whitaker's Almanack, published annually by J. Whitaker, London

Wills and Their Whereabouts, by A. J. Camp, Phillimore, Chichester, 1974

Wills and Where to Find Them, by J. S. W. Gibson, Phillimore, Chichester, 1974

8

Specialist Research

While the writer will always find it more rewarding to undertake his own research, and should do so whenever feasible, there are times when it pays to employ the expert. Books or records to be consulted may be accessible only at some distance from the writer's home; specialist knowledge of a subject may be required, or knowledge of local records which it would take the inexperienced researcher, or one from another district, months, if not years, to acquire – in such events the employment of an expert will usually save the client time and money in the long term. If he has press deadlines looming, or other commitments, it may even pay him to off-load some of the more routine research as well.

Writers wishing to get in touch with a freelance researcher will find some names listed in the *Writers' and Artists' Yearbook*, under 'Editorial, Literary and Production Services', and in the Cassell and Publishers Association *Directory of Publishing*, under 'Trade and Allied Services: publishing consultancies and research services in Great Britain'. The British Library Reference Division, the Public Record Office and some other libraries and local record offices maintain lists of researchers/record agents and will pass on names and addresses to enquirers (send a stamped addressed envelope); naturally, they do not accept any responsibility for the work undertaken by these people. Experts willing to do research may also sometimes be contacted through the secretaries or librarians of professional or trade societies or institutions; alternatively, an advertisement in a professional or trade journal may yield a suitable result. Some freelancers advertise their service in *The Times*, the *Times Literary Supplement*, *The Author*, *Books and Bookman*, and similar papers. Schoolmasters and university students often seek research assignments during the long vacation. For details of how to obtain the services of a qualified indexer, see page 147.

Contacting a suitable researcher abroad is rather more difficult. You can write to the national library of the country concerned, or to the library or archives centre where you want the research to be done (always enclose a sufficient number of International Reply Coupons for airmail if writing overseas – one is not enough); or you can approach the cultural attaché of the relevant embassy, legation or High Commission in London. Some names and addresses of American and Canadian researchers and agencies will be found in Appendix 3 of *Fee-Based Information Services* by Lorig Maranjian and Richard W. Boss (New York and London: Bowker, 1980).

The most obvious occasions when a writer may need this kind of help are in the fields of genealogy, when a complicated ancestral search may be necessary for the first chapter of a biography; in local or family history, for which not only a knowledge of the classes of records available is required, but also some skill in reading Latin and transcribing old handwriting; in picture research; and in translation.

Genealogy

Experience in palaeography and genealogy is acquired only after considerable study, and there are many traps into which the unwary novice can fall. A working knowledge of Latin is essential for the study of medieval or earlier texts, while later source material demands the ability to read and transcribe both the 'secretary hand' (the script in use in England from the mid-16th to the mid-17th centuries) and the later 'court hand', each with distinctive forms of capital letters and contractions. Unless you are embarking on your family or local history as a hobby, therefore, and can afford the time to qualify yourself in these subjects, some professional assistance will be desirable.

It is wise to employ someone who lives in the area in which the relevant search is to be made, for he will be familiar both with the local records and with local family names, and thus can save the client time and money. Most local record offices maintain lists of recommended searchers; alternatively, names and addresses of professional genealogists and record agents who are members of the Association of Genealogists and Record Agents (AGRA) may be obtained from the Hon. Secretary, Mrs Jean Tooke, 1 Woodside Close, Caterham, Surrey CR3 6AU (send a stamped addressed envelope, 60p for UK, or 5 International Reply Coupons for overseas mailing). All AGRA members have satisfied the Council as to their integrity, qualifications and experience, and they adhere to a strict professional code.

The College of Arms (Queen Victoria Street, London EC4V 4BT) is open to enquiries of a genealogical and heraldic nature from the public (Arms and pedigrees of English, Northern Irish and Commonwealth families) and will carry out research in connection with the right to Arms for clients on a fee-paying basis. Debrett Ancestry Research (67 Parchment Street, Winchester SO23 8AT), which formerly catered only for royalty and the aristocracy, now offers a worldwide genealogical research service to the commoner; and among other professional firms who will undertake genealogical work are Achievements Ltd (Northgate, Canterbury, Kent CT1 1BA). The latter, who are associated with the Institute of Heraldic and Genealogical Studies (at the same address), will also accept art-work commissions (family trees, coats of arms, heraldic designs, etc.). Advertisements of firms and individuals offering genealogical research services in various regions of this country and abroad will be found in the *Genealogists' Magazine*, the quarterly journal of the Society of Genealogists. The Society will itself carry out research, on behalf of members and non-members; enquiries, accompanied by a stamped addressed envelope, should be addressed to the Director of Research, The Society of Genealogists, 14 Charterhouse Buildings, London EC1M 7BA.

Picture Research

Picture research is an immensely complicated field and therefore beyond the scope of this handbook. Sometimes a writer will be expected to provide all the illustrative material for his book or article; in other cases the publisher will employ a professional picture researcher, who may be a member of his staff or a freelance, to locate and select pictures, commission photographers, and clear the copyright and reproduction fees on a particular project. Whether the author or the publisher foots the bill for the picture researcher is a matter for negotiation. But a wise author makes sure that it is stipulated in his contract that it will be the publisher who bears responsibility for print and reproduction fees, since these can be very costly.

Writers wishing to obtain the services of a qualified picture researcher are recommended to contact the freelance register of the Society of Picture Researchers and Editors (SPREd): telephone Miranda Smith on 01-520 0956. For other information about the Society, write or telephone to SPREd, BM Box 259, London WC1N 3XX (tel. 01-404 5011).

For those who are tempted to do their own picture research and need a good introduction to the subject, the *Writers' & Artists' Yearbook*, published annually by A & C Black, contains an excellent article by Judith Harries. Among a variety of useful manuals and source-books are the following:

Art of Picture Research, The, by Hilary and Mary Evans, David & Charles, Newton Abbot, 1979

BAPLA Directory, published annually by the British Association of Picture Libraries and Agencies, PO Box 4, Andoversford, Cheltenham, Glos.

Directory of British Photographic Collections ed. J. Wall, Heinemann, London, on behalf of the Royal Photographic Society, 1977

Picture Researcher's Handbook, The, by Hilary and Mary Evans and Andra Nelke, David & Charles, Newton Abbot, 1975; 3rd edition due in 1986 from Van Nostrand Reinhold

Picture Source Book for Social History, 6 vols, Allen & Unwin, London, 1961

Picture Sources UK: A Guide to more than 1200 Public and Private Picture Collections, Macdonald, London, 1985 (to be updated regularly)

Sources of Illustration 1500-1900, Adams & Dart, London, 1971

Translation

Translation is another field in which professional help may be required from time to time. For basic research purposes a rough translation or précis may be adequate to work on, but any passage to be quoted in print should be prepared by a qualified translator. The best way to find one is to apply to the Translators' Guild Ltd (part of the Institute of Linguists), 24A Highbury Grove, London N5 2EA (tel. 01-359 7445), stating the languages from and into which the translation will be required and also the subject-matter. If the Guild cannot provide one of its own members to undertake the commission, it will endeavour to put the enquirer in touch with a suitable person. Alternatively, translation agencies may be located in the yellow pages of most telephone directories.

The Translator's Handbook by Catriona Picken (Aslib, London, 1983) is an excellent introduction and source-book for all members of the profession; it will also be of use to writers who need to commission a translator.

Research Fees

Fees for professional freelance assistance are negotiable and depend on the nature and complexity of the task. Genealogists, record agents and researchers usually work on an hourly basis plus out-of-pocket expenses (travelling, search fees, photocopying, postages, telephone, etc.); short pieces of translation are charged per thousand words. Most freelance workers have a sliding scale of fees; the professional bodies to which the majority of them belong recommend standard rates for the job, and if you are asked to pay 'above the odds' it will be either because the assignment is very specialised or complicated, or needed in a great rush (necessitating week-end and evening work), or because the person engaged has special qualifications.

It is normal practice for the client commissioning the work to pay a lump sum on account (up to 50% of the total cost estimated) and the balance on completion, but in the case of long-term commissions accounts may be rendered monthly. Estimates will be given on request; but do not expect your researcher to give one with any accuracy – neither he nor you will know at the outset precisely how much time he will spend on the job.

Fees paid to researchers, genealogists, translators and other workers may be set against a writer's tax.

9

Information from Foreign Sources

The British writer who needs to use foreign sources – published or unpublished documentary material – or to obtain background information on other countries should first of all explore what is available in the United Kingdom. All the copyright libraries and major reference libraries here have substantial foreign language holdings, and there should be little difficulty encountered in obtaining most standard works.

National encyclopedias, bibliographies and current works of reference are usually to be found on the open shelves. If these do not provide what you are looking for, you should next consult the library's subject index, first under the relevant country and then under the desired subject sub-heading.

The principal foreign newspapers and weeklies going back many years are held at the British Library Newspaper Library in Colindale, although there are some gaps during the two world wars; nowadays most are purchased on microfilm. The whereabouts of foreign periodicals in British libraries can be traced in the *British Union-Catalogue of Periodicals*. Current publications worldwide are listed in *Benn's Media Directory* and *Ulrich's International Periodicals Directory*; *Willing's Press Guide* covers the United Kingdom, Europe, the United States, the Gulf States, Australasia and the Far East.

Annual subscriptions to foreign newspapers and periodicals can be arranged, with payment in sterling, through firms such as Bailey Subscription Agents Ltd, Dept W6, Warner House, Folkestone, Kent CT19 6PH (tel. Folkestone (0303) 56501) or Dawson's, Cannon House, Folkestone, Kent CT19 5EE (tel. Folkestone (0303) 57421). The Dawson Book Service and Bailey Bros & Swinfen Ltd (address as for Bailey Subscription Agents, above-mentioned), import foreign books; the latter firm also offers a search service for out-of-print foreign titles.

The use of bibliographies and how to trace books has been dealt with earlier in this handbook (see pages 29-37). In Walford's *Guide to Reference Material* and its US equivalent, Sheehy's *Guide to Reference Books* (details in chapter 3), encyclopedias, national bibliographies and major works are listed, subject by subject, under the relevant sub-heading of each country. For quick factual reference the following single-volume mini-encyclopedias are recommended additions to the writer's own bookshelf: *Le Petit Larousse* (French); *Der Brockhaus in einem Band* (German); *Pequeño Larousse Illustrado* (Spanish). It is always worthwhile keeping an eye open for these as they appear (they are updated regularly), and you can often pick them up secondhand: some of the information they contain is not always included in English language encyclopedias. It goes without saying that if you are using foreign sources you will need at least a working (reading) knowledge of the language or languages concerned; otherwise you must be prepared to go to the considerable expense of translation. A series of good foreign-language/English dictionaries is essential, along with the basic grammars.

Tourist information offices (listed in the London telephone directory) will provide up-to-date travel and basic background material on foreign countries, while the press offices of the relevant embassies and High Commissions, or the cultural attachés (names and addresses in the current *London Diplomatic List*, published quarterly by HMSO and available at most library enquiry desks) are usually extremely helpful, either with specific problems or in suggesting where you should address your enquiries in the country concerned. Public relations officers of the major international companies may also provide useful source material; names and addresses will be found in the current *Hollis Press & Public Relations Annual*.

There are biographical dictionaries for most countries, and up-to-date biographical information will be found in the *Who's Who* of the country concerned; where no publications exist for the country in which you are interested, it is best to ask the relevant embassy or High Commission in London.

Details of foreign libraries in the United Kingdom will be found in the *Aslib Directory*. The researcher who lives in or near London will be able to make use of the following:

Bibliothèque de l'Institut Français, 15 Queensberry Place, London SW7 2DT (tel. 01-589 6211). Use of reference facilities is free; books may be borrowed on subscription. Open Mon. – Fri., 11 – 6.

German Institute Library, 50-51 Princes Gate, London SW7 2PG (tel. 01-581 3344). Open to the public, free of charge, for reference and study, Mon. – Thurs., 10 – 8; Sat., 10 – 1.

India Office Library and Records, 197 Blackfriars Road, London

SE1 8NG (tel. 01-928 9531). Open Mon. – Fri., 9.30 – 5.45; Sat.,
9.30 – 12.45. Newspaper reading room at Bush House, Aldwych,
London WC2B 4PH, open only Tues., Thurs., 10 – 5.30.

Institute of Commonwealth Studies Library, 27-28 Russell Square,
London WC1B 5DS (tel. 01-580 5876). Open (during term) Mon.
– Wed., 10 – 7, Thurs., Fri., 10 – 6; (during vacations), Mon. –
Fri., 10 – 5.30.

Institute of Spain Library, 102 Eaton Square, London SW1 9AN (tel.
01-235 1485). Open to non-members for reference use, Mon. –
Fri., 10 – 6 (during term), 10 – 3 (during vacations).

Royal Commonwealth Society Library, Northumberland Avenue,
London WC2N 5BJ (tel. 01-930 6733). Open to members and to
bona fide researchers, Mon. – Fri., 10 – 5.30.

School of Oriental and African Studies Library, Malet Street,
London WC1E 7HP (tel. 01-637 2388). Open (during term) Mon.
– Thurs., 9 – 8, Fri., 9 – 6.30; (during vacations), Mon. – Fri., 9 –
5; Sats. (term and vacation), 9.30 – 12.30.

United States of America Information Service Library, American
Embassy, 24 Grosvenor Square, London W1A 1AE (tel. 01-499
7060). Open Mon.-Fri., 10-12, 2-4.

When material cannot be located in this country and it is necessary
to make enquiries at libraries or research institutions abroad, it is not
only good manners but will also avoid possible confusion or delay at
the other end if you have your initial letter professionally translated.
(For details of how to find translation services, see page 122.) If any
extensive research is involved, the foreign librarian or archivist will
usually be able to put you in touch with a local freelance researcher.

The leading libraries abroad are listed in *The World of Learning*,
published by Europa, London, and in two excellent guides by Helga
Lengenfelder: *World Guide to Libraries* and *World Guide to Special
Libraries*, both published by Saur, Munich, 1983 (distributed in the
UK by the Library Association, London). Another useful guide is J.
Burkett's *Library and Information Networks in W. Europe*, Aslib,
London, 1983. The two Bowker annuals, *Literary Market Place* and
International Literary Market Place, covering the United States and
the rest of the world respectively, are good sources of information on
libraries and the book trade generally, with reference books,
periodicals, literary associations and prizes detailed under individual
countries.

The best place to look initially for information on foreign
countries is in the *World Bibliographical Series* published by Clio
Press of Oxford: this is an ongoing series in which already more than
50 volumes have appeared. There is also an excellent series on

International Historical Statistics (separate volumes for Europe; Africa and Asia; The Americas and Australasia) published by Macmillan, London. A good historical source is the multi-volume *Guide to the Sources for the History of the Nations* series, published by Saur, Munich, for the International Council on Archives (ICA). *Archivum, The International Review on Archives*, published by the ICA, is also of interest: volumes 22/23 constitute an International Directory of Archives, up to date at January 1975, while the more recent volume 30 (summer 1984) is an index to the previous 29 volumes and contains a great deal of information on archives, libraries, museums and information centres throughout the world.

Space does not permit the examination in any detail of specific foreign sources or guides to sources, of which there are many. However, as a guideline to researchers who are interested in this field, a selection of libraries and source-books for the United States and for France are given below, followed by shorter lists for some other countries.

United States of America

The Library of Congress, Washington DC (tel. (202) 287-5000) is the national library, but it is not the exact equivalent of the British Library in that it does not automatically acquire a copy of every book published in the United States; it does, however, collect and catalogue books published in all countries. The *National Union Catalog*, which has replaced the old *Library of Congress Catalog*, is on the open shelves of the British Library Reading Room and in larger UK libraries. The *Pre-1956 Imprints*, an impressive run of 755 volumes, are very clear and easy to use, and their great value to the researcher is that they provide in one alphabetical sequence, under authors, the holdings of the Library of Congress together with those of the principal libraries of North America.

Among other major US libraries are:

Beinecke Rare Book and Manuscript Library, Yale University, Box 1603A, Yale Station, New Haven, Conn. 06520 (tel. (203) 436-8438)

Chicago Historical Society Library, North Avenue and Clark Street, Chicago, Ill. 60614 (tel. (312) 642-4600)

Chicago Public Library, 425 North Michigan Avenue, Chicago, Ill. 60611 (tel. (312) 269-2900)

Free Library of Philadelphia, Logan Square, Philadelphia, Pa. 19103 (tel. (215) 686-5322)

Harvard University Library, Cambridge, Mass. 02138 (tel. (617)
495-2401)
Huntington Library, San Marino, California 91108 (tel. (818)
405-2100)
National Archives and Records Service, National Archives Building,
8th Street at Pennsylvania Avenue NW, Washington DC 20408
(tel. (202) 523-3218)
National Geographic Society Library, 17th and M Streets NW,
Washington DC 20036 (tel. (202) 857-7787)
New York Historical Society, 170 Central Park West, New York,
NY 10024 (tel. (212) 873-3400)
New York Public Library, Fifth Avenue and 42nd Street, New York,
NY 10018 (tel. (212) 930-0744)
Pierpont Morgan Library, 29 East 36th Street, New York, NY
10016 (tel. (212) 685-0008)
Smithsonian Institution, National Museum of Natural History
Building, 10th and Constitution Avenue NW, Washington DC
20560 (tel. (202) 357-2139)
Stanford University Libraries, Stanford, California 94305 (tel. (415)
497-2016)
United Nations Library – Dag Hammarskjöld Library, United
Nations Plaza, New York, NY 10017 (tel. (212) 754-7412)
Yale University Library, New Haven, Conn. 06520 (tel. (203)
436-8335)

Recommended reference works:

Ayer Directory of Publications, published annually by Ayer Press,
Philadelphia
Books in Print, published annually by Bowker, New York; also
Subject Guide to Books in Print
Collier's Encyclopedia, 24 vols, Macmillan Education Corporation.
New York, 1981
Dictionary of American Biography, 21 vols + 6 supplements,
(covering period up to 1960), Scribner, New York, 1928-80
Encyclopedia of Associations, 5 vols, published annually by Gale
Research, Detroit
Facts on File, published weekly since 1940 by Facts on File, New
York, with regular consolidations
Guide to Manuscripts relating to America in the United Kingdom,
ed. John W. Raimo, Mansell, London, 1979
Guide to Reference Books, by E. P. Sheehy, American Library
Association, Chicago, 1976; supplements, 1980, 1982, 1984
Information Please Almanac, published annually since 1947 by
Simon and Schuster, New York

Introduction to Reference Work, 2 vols, by William Katz, McGraw Hill, New York, 1982

National Inventory of Documentary Sources in the United States, on microfiche, four parts (Part 1 *Federal Records* and Part 2 *Manuscript Division, Library of Congress*, each updated twice a year; Part 3 *State Archives, Libraries and Historical Societies;* and Part 4 *Academic Libraries and Other Repositories*, 5 units per year with cumulating index, Chadwyck-Healey, Cambridge

North American Online Directory, The, Bowker, New York, 1985

Oxford Companion to American History, Oxford University Press, 1966

Statistical Abstract of the United States, published annually since 1879 by the Government Printing Office, Washington DC

Who was Who in America, 1897-1981, 7 vols, 1942-81; *Historical volume* (1607-1896), 1963; *Index volume* (1607-1981), 1981 Marquis, Chicago

Who's Who in America, published biennially in 2 vols by Marquis, Chicago

At the British Library Newspaper Library in Colindale there are on the open shelves indexes to the *New York Times* (from 1851), *Washington Post* (from 1955), *Chicago Tribune* (from 1972), and to some other American papers; also *Union List of American Newspapers* and *Latin American Newspapers in US Libraries*.

France

The national library is the Bibliothèque Nationale, 58 rue de Richelieu, 75002 Paris (tel. 4261.82.83). It publishes a *Catalogue général des livres imprimés* (printed books), a *Catalogue général des manuscrits français* (manuscripts) and a *Catalogue collectif des périodiques* (periodicals), plus two concise guides to the printed books and manuscripts collections respectively. Researchers visiting the Bibliothèque Nationale (known to scholars in France as the '*BN*') may obtain, free of charge, at the enquiry desk a booklet entitled *Bibliothèques specialisées de Paris et région Parisienne (selectionnés par matières)*, a useful guide to specialist libraries in and around the city. An annex to the *BN*, housing newspapers and periodicals, was opened in 1981 at Provins, east of Paris.

Among other libraries and archive collections (but excluding the Paris and other university libraries, which are too numerous to mention) are:

Archives Nationales, 60 rue des Francs-Bourgeois, 75003 Paris (tel. 4277.11.30)

Bibliothèque de l'Arsenal, 1 rue Sully, 75004 Paris (tel. 4277.44.21)

Bibliothèque Centrale du Muséum National d'Histoire Naturelle, 38 rue Geoffroy St Hilaire, 75005 Paris (tel. 4331.71.24)

Bibliothèque de la Documentation Française, 29-31 quai Voltaire, 75007 Paris (tel. 4261.50.10) (Also sells *Archives Nationales* publications.)

Bibliothèque de l'Institut de France, 23 quai Conti, 75006 Paris (tel. 4326.85.40)

Bibliothèque du Centre National d'Art et de Culture Georges Pompidou, 19 rue Beaubourg, 75004 Paris (tel. 4277.12.33) This excellent reference library at the Centre Beaubourg has been growing fast in recent years and contains many books hitherto available only at the *BN*; it is open daily from 10 to 6, and the staff are most cooperative (but some knowledge of French is necessary, especially if you are making enquiries by telephone).

Bibliothèque Forney, l'Hôtel de Sens, 1 rue du Figuier, 75004 Paris (tel. 4278.14.60)

Bibliothèque Historique de la Ville de Paris, 24 rue Pavée, 75004 Paris (tel. 4274.44.44)

Bibliothèque Mazarine, 23 quai Conti, 75006 Paris (tel. 4354.89.48)

Bibliothèque Sainte-Geneviève, 10 place du Panthéon, 75005 Paris (tel. 4329.61.00)

Recommended reference works:

Annuaire Statistique de la France, published annually by I.N.S.E.E., Paris

Archives Nationales, Les, 3 vols to date, published by La Documentation Française, Paris, 1978, 1980

Bottin Administratif (yearbook of government departments and public offices), Didot-Bottin, Paris, annually

Dictionnaire de biographie française, Letouzey, Paris, 1929- (in progress)

Grand Larousse Encyclopédique, 10 vols, Larousse, Paris, 1960-64; supplements, 1968, 1975

How to Find Out about France, by J. E. Pemberton, Pergamon, Oxford, 1966

Libraries in France, by John Ferguson, Bingley, London, 1971 (The above two titles are now out of print and to some extent out of date; but they still contain much useful information.)

Livres Hebdo: Bibliographie de la France, published weekly, with monthly and quarterly supplements, by Éditions Professionelles du Livre, Paris, since 1979. (This has superseded the earlier *Bibliographie de la France*, published since 1811, and *Biblio*, since 1933.)

Répertoire des Bibliothèques et Organismes de Documentation, Bibliothèque Nationale, Paris, vol 1, 1971; vol 2, 1973

Who's Who in France, published biennially (in French) since 1953 by Éditions Jacques Lafitte, Paris

The Press Office of the French Embassy in London issues a compact publication, regularly updated (3rd edition, 1985): *France, A Journalist's Guide*, which is available free on request. Anyone who has to do research in or about France will find this invaluable.

Short List of Other Foreign Source-material (arranged alphabetically under area or country)

Africa

Sources of information in the UK:

International African Institute, Lionel Robbins Building, 10 Portugal Street, London WC2A 2HD (tel. 01-405 7686)

School of Oriental and African Studies, University of London, Malet Street, London WC1E 7HP (tel. 01-637 2388)

Recommended books:

Africa South of the Sahara 1984-5, Europa Publications, London, 1984

Africa Today and *Africa Who's Who*, both published by Africa Journal Group, London

African Book World and Press, The; a directory, published by Saur, Munich, 1984

African Books in Print, 3rd ed., 2 vols, Mansell, London, 1983

African Political Facts since 1945, ed. C. Cook and D. Killingray, Macmillan, London, 1983

Dictionary of African Historical Biography, ed. M. R. Lipschutz and R. K. Rasmussen, Heinemann, London, 1978

Dictionary of South African Biography, BPK, Cape Town, 1968- (in progress)

Guide to Materials for West African History in European Archives, 5 vols, Institute of Historical Research, London, 1965-73

International African Bibliography, published quarterly since 1971 by Mansell, London, with regular cumulative volumes

New African Yearbook, 3 vols: Central and Southern Africa; West and Central Africa; Nigeria, East and Southern Africa, IC Publications, London, updated annually

South African Bibliography to the year 1925, 4 vols, Mansell, London, 1979 (revision and continuation of Mendelssohn's *South African Bibliography*, 1910)

Statistics Africa, CBD Research, Beckenham, Kent, updated every few years

Theses on Africa accepted by Universities in the United Kingdom and Ireland 1920-1962, Heffer, Cambridge, on behalf of Standing Conference on Library Materials on Africa, 1964; *Theses on Africa . . . 1963-1975*, compiled by J. H. StJ. McIlwaine, Mansell, London, 1978

Year Book of the Republic of South Africa, published annually by the South African Department of Information

Arab States and the Middle East

Sources of information in the UK:

Arab League Information Centre, 52 Green Street, London W1Y 3RH (tel. 01-629 0732)

Institute of Arabic and Islamic Studies, University of Lancaster, Bailrigg, Lancaster LA1 4YH (tel. Lancaster (0524) 65201)

Middle East Centre, St Antony's College, Oxford OX2 6JF (tel. Oxford (0865) 259651 ext. 64). (Collections of papers of individuals involved in the Middle East from 1800 to the present day).

Recommended books:

Book World Directory of the Arab Countries, Turkey and Iran, compiled by A. Rudkin and I. Butcher, Mansell, London, 1979

Index Islamicus 1906-1955, with 4 supplements to 1975 (published every 5 years), Mansell, London, 1958-78; 5th supplement (1976-1980), 2 vols, 1983; *Index* published quarterly since 1977

International Who's Who of the Arab World, published in London, alternate years

Middle East and North Africa 1984-5, The, Europa Publications, London, 1984

Saudi Arabia: A Bibliography on Politics, Society and Economics from the 18th Century to the Present, by H. J. Philipp, Saur, Munich, 1984

Union Catalogue of Arab Serials and Newspapers in British Libraries, ed. P. Auchterlonie and Y. H. Safadi, Mansell, London, 1977 (indexed in English and Arabic)

Who's Who in Saudi Arabia 1983-4, Europa Publications, London, 1984

Who's Who in the Arab World 1984/5, Bowker, New York, 1984

Asia and the Far East

Sources of information in the UK:

Central Asian Research Centre, 8 Wakley Street, London EC1V 7LT (tel. 01-278 9441); part of collection transferred to Society for Central Asian Studies, 19A Paradise Street, Oxford OX1 1LD (tel. Oxford (0865) 249841)

Centre of South Asian Studies, University of Cambridge, Laundress Lane, Cambridge CB2 1SD (tel. Cambridge (0223) 65621 ext. 202)

School of Oriental and African Studies, University of London, Malet Street, London WC1E 7HP (tel. 01-637 2388)

Recommended books:

Asia: a selected and annotated guide to reference works, by G. R. Nunn, MIT Press, Cambridge, Mass., 1971

Books on Asia, from the Near East to the Far East: a guide for the general reader, by E. Birnbaum, University of Toronto Press, 1971

Cumulative bibliography of Asian Studies 1941-1965, 8 vols: *1966-1970*, 8 vols, Association for Asian Studies Inc., Boston, Mass., 1969-72; also annually

Far East and Australasia 1984-85, The, Europa Publications, London, 1984

Government Archives in S. Asia, ed. D. A. Low, J. C. Iltis and M. D. Wainwright, Cambridge University Press, 1969

Statistics Asia and Australasia, CBD Research, Beckenham, Kent, updated every few years

The Commonwealth

Sources of information in the UK:

Institute of Commonwealth Studies, 27-28 Russell Square, London WC1B 5DS (tel. 01-580 5876)

Institute of Commonwealth Studies, Oxford University, Queen

Elizabeth House, 21 St Giles, Oxford OX1 3LA (tel. Oxford (0865) 52952)

Royal Commonwealth Society, Northumberland Avenue, London WC2N 5BJ (tel. 01-930 6733)

Researchers should also contact the various High Commissions in London, i.e. Australia House, Canada House, India House, New Zealand House, etc. (addresses and telephone numbers in *Whitaker's Almanack* under 'The Commonwealth' or in *Hollis Press & Public Relations Annual* under 'International and Overseas Information Sources in the UK', and the London telephone directory).

Recommended books:

General

Commonwealth Political Facts, ed. Chris Cook, Macmillan, London, 1979

Who's Who in the Commonwealth, International Biographical Centre, Cambridge, updated regularly

Yearbook of the Commonwealth, HMSO, London, annually

Note: The Library of the Institute of Commonwealth Studies in London (see above) publishes a quarterly *Accessions List* and an annual list of *Theses in Progress in Commonwealth Studies*; it also maintains a card catalogue of completed theses.

Australia

Australian Books in Print 1984, Bowker, New York

Australian Dictionary of Biography, Melbourne University Press: Period I (*1788-1850*), 2 vols; Period II (*1851-1890*), 4 vols; Period III (*1891-1939*), 3 vols published to date, 3 vols to come

Australian National Bibliography, National Library of Australia, Canberra (previously known as *Annual Catalogue of Australian Publications*, published 1936-1960): since 1972 published weekly, with monthly and 4-monthly cumulations and annual volumes

Official Year Book of the Commonwealth of Australia, published annually by the Government Printing Office, Canberra

Who's Who in Australia, published triennially since 1906 by the *Herald and Weekly Times*, Melbourne

Canada

Canadian Reference Sources: A Selective Guide, rev. ed., ed. D. E. Ryder, Canadian Library Association, Ottawa, 1981

Canadiana, national bibliography published monthly since 1951, with annual cumulations, National Library of Canada, Ottawa

Dictionary of Canadian Biography, University of Toronto Press, 1966- (in progress)

Encyclopedia Canadiana (standard national encyclopedia). A new *Canadian Encyclopedia*, was published by Hurtig in 3 volumes in September 1985

Historical Statistics of Canada, ed. M. C. Urquhart and K. A. H. Buckley, Macmillan, London, 1965

How to Find Out about Canada, by H. C. Campbell, Pergamon, Oxford, 1967 (out of print, but contains useful information)

Statistics Canada, published annually by the Information Department of Canada, Ottawa

Who's Who in Canada, published annually since 1907 by Toronto International Press

India

Index India, published quarterly by Rajasthan University, Jaipur, since 1967

India: A Reference Manual, published annually since 1953 by the Ministry of Information and Broadcasting, New Delhi

India Who's Who, published annually since 1969 by INFA Publications, New Delhi

Indian National Bibliography, published monthly, with annual cumulations, since 1958 by the Central Reference Library, Calcutta

New Zealand

Bibliography of New Zealand Bibliographies, New Zealand Library Association, Wellington, 1967

Books and Pamphlets relating to Culture and the Arts in New Zealand, compiled by B. Smyth and H. Howorth, Christchurch, 1978

Encyclopedia of New Zealand, ed. A. H. McLintock, 3 vols, Owen, Wellington, 1966

Guide to New Zealand Reference Material, 2nd ed., compiled by J. Harris, New Zealand Library Association, Wellington, 1950; supplements 1951-57

New Zealand National Bibliography, monthly since 1967, National Library of New Zealand, Wellington

New Zealand Official Year Book, published annually by the Department of Statistics, Wellington

Regrettably, space does not permit the listing of other Commonwealth countries in this section.

Europe

Given the vast amount of material published each year, readers will understand that it is impossible to do more in the space of this chapter than to list some of the countries of Europe, with the location of their national libraries/archives and a selection of reference works (by title only). There are, however, a number of general guides which should first be mentioned. These include:

Directory of European Associations, 2 vols: I *Trade, Industrial and Professional Associations*, 1986; II *National, Learned and Scientific Societies*, 1984, CBD Research, Beckenham, Kent, updated very 4 years

European Historical Statistics, 1750-1975, 2nd ed., ed. B. R. Mitchell, Macmillan, London, 1980

European Political Facts, 4 vols, covering period 1648-1948, Macmillan, London, 1978-85

European Sources of Scientific and Technical Information, 6th ed., ed. A. P. Harvey, Longman, 1985

New Guide to the Diplomatic Archives of Western Europe, ed. D. H. Thomas and L. M. Case, University of Pennsylvania Press, 1975

Official Publications of Western Europe, ed. E. Johansson, Mansell, London, vol 1 only to date, 1984

Statistics Europe, CBD Research, Beckenham, Kent, updated regularly

Who's Who in Europe, Servi-Tech, Brussels, updated irregularly (latest edition, 6 th, 1985)

Note: For purposes of this chapter, 'Europe' refers to Western Europe. The countries of Eastern Europe are included under the heading 'USSR and Eastern Europe'.

Austria

The Österreichische Nationalbibliothek in Vienna is the national library, and there is also the Staatsarchiv (national archives) in the same city.

Austria, facts and figures
Dokumentation und Information in Österreich
Österreichische Bibliographie
Österreichisches Biographisches Lexikon 1815-1950
Österreich Lexikon
Who's Who in Austria

Belgium

The Bibliothèque royale Albert Ier/Koninklijke Bibliotheek Albert I and the Archives générales du Royaume, both in Brussels, are the major library and archive sources.
Bibliographie de Belge/Belgische bibliografie
Documentation sur la Belgique: bibliographie sélective et analytique
Inventaire des centres belges de recherche
Who's Who in Belgium and the Grand Duchy of Luxembourg

Denmark – see under 'Scandinavia'

Germany

The two major libraries in the Federal Republic are the Deutsche Bibliothek in Frankfurt and the Staatsbibliothek Prüssischer Kulturbesitz in West Berlin; The Deutsche Staatsbibliothek (formerly the Prüssische Staatsbibliothek) is now the national library of the German Democratic Republic.
Allgemeine Deutsche Biographie
Der Grosse Brockhaus (encyclopedia)
Deutsche Bibliographie (Federal Republic of Germany)
Deutsche Nationalbibliographie (German Democratic Republic)
Germany (FRG), Statistical Sources
Libraries in the Federal Republic of Germany
Neue Deutsche Biographie
Verzeichnis der Spezialbibliotheken in der Bundesrepublik Deutschland (list of special libraries in the Federal Republic including West Berlin)
Wer ist Wer? (includes some Austrian and Swiss entries)
Who's Who in Germany

Greece

The National Library is in Athens.
Greek Bibliography
Guide to Greek Libraries and Cultural Organizations
Hellenika Vivla (bibliography)
Modern Greece: A Bibliography
Mega Hellenikon Biographikon Lexikon (biographical dictionary), in progress

Italy

The major libraries are the Biblioteca Nazionale Centrale Vittorio

Emanuele II in Rome and the Biblioteca Nazionale Centrale in Florence; there are also national libraries in Milan, Naples, Palermo, Turin and Venice.

Bibliografia Nazionale Italiana
Dizionario Biografico degli Italiani
Enciclopedia Italiana di Scienze, Lettre ed Arti
Guida delle Bibliothece Italiane
How to Find Out about Italy
Lui, Chi, E?
Who's Who in Italy

The Netherlands

The major collection is at the Koninklijke Bibliotheek (Royal Library) in The Hague; nearby, in Voorburg, there is the Centraal Bureau voor de Statistiek.

Brinkman's Cumulatieve Catalogus van Boeken (bibliography)
Digest of the Kingdom of the Netherlands (Government Information Service publication)
Grote Nederlandse Larousse Encyclopedie
Grote Winkler Prins Encyclopedie
Nieuw Nederlandsch Biografisch Woordenboek
Who's Who in the Netherlands
Wie is Dat?

Norway – see under 'Scandinavia'

Scandinavia

Two biographical dictionaries covering the region are the *Dictionary of Scandinavian Biography* and *Who's Who in Scandinavia*; the latter publication (1st ed., Bowker, New York, 1981) includes an appendix listing societies, associations and institutions.

Denmark

The Kongelige Bibliotek (Royal Library) in Copenhagen is the national library; the archive collection is at the Kobenhavns Stadsarkiv.

Bibliography of Books on Denmark 1900-1965
Dansk Biografisk Leksikon
Dansk Bogfortegnelse (national bibliography)
Denmark: An Official Handbook
Denmark: A Select Bibliography
Who's Who in Denmark

Norway

The national library is the Universitetsbiblioteket i Oslo (Royal University Library), and the national archives are at the Riksarkivet, also in Oslo.

Facts about Norway
Guide to Norwegian Statistics
Hvem or Hvem? (Norwegian who's who)
Norsk Biografisk Leksikon
Norsk Bokfortegnelse (national bibliography)
Norway Year Book

Sweden

The Kungliga Biblioteket (Royal Library), the Riksarkivet (National Record Office) and the Statistika Centralbyráns Bibliteket (Library of Statistics) are all in Stockholm.

Facts about Sweden
Svenskt Biografiskt Lexikon
Svensk Bokforteckning (national bibliography)
Vem är Det? (Swedish who's who)

Spain

The Biblioteca Nacional is in Madrid, as are the Archivo General de la Administracion Civil del Estado (the General Archives of the Civil Administration of the State) and the Archivo Historico Nacional (the National Historical Archives). There is also the Real Biblioteca (Royal Library) at El Escorial, near Madrid. The Archivo de la Corona de Aragon (the Royal Archives of Aragon) are in Barcelona, where there is also the Biblioteca de Catalunya (the Library of Catalonia).

Bibliografía Española
Enciclopedia Universal Ilustrada Europeo-Americana
Gran Enciclopedia Rialp
Indice Cultural Español (Spanish cultural index)
Quién es quién (Spanish who's who)
Who's Who in Spain

Switzerland

The national library is the Schweizerische Landesbibliothek/Bibliothèque Nationale Suisse in Berne; the Archives Fédérales (national archives) are in the same city. In Geneva there are the United Nations Library and the International Labour Office Library.

Das Schweizer Buch/Le Livre Suisse (national bibliography)
Swiss Who's Who

For the remaining areas of the world – Latin America and the Caribbean, the USSR and Eastern Europe – space does not permit the inclusion of major libraries in all the different countries. A short list of bibliographies and general works is therefore given under each of these two sections, which should be useful to the researcher.

Latin America and the Caribbean

Bibliografia Latinoamericana, CERLAL, Bogotá, 1974-
Cambridge Encyclopedia of Latin America and the Caribbean, ed. H. Blakemore, S. Collier and T. Skidmore, Cambridge University Press, 1985
Caribbeana, 1900-1965: a topical bibliography, by L. Comitas, University of Washington Press, Seattle and London, 1968
CARICOM Bibliography, Caricom Secretariat, Georgetown, Guyana, 1977-
South America, Central America and the Caribbean 1986, Europa Publications, London, 1985
South American Handbook, The, published annually since 1924 by Trade & Travel Publications, London
West Indies & Caribbean Year Book, The, published annually by Thomas Skinner Directories, East Grinstead, W. Sussex

USSR and Eastern Europe

Archives and Manuscript Repositories in the USSR, Estonia, Latvia, Lithuania and Byelorussia, by Patricia Kennedy Grimsted, Princeton University Press, N.J., 1981
Great Soviet Encyclopedia, The, (translation of *Bol'shaya Sovetskaya Entsiklopediya*, 3rd edition), 30 vols, Macmillan, New York and Collier-Macmillan, London, 1973-82
Guide to Russian Reference Books, Stanford University, California, 1962- (in progress)
Information Bulgaria, Pergamon, Oxford, 1985
Information USSR, Pergamon, Oxford, 1962
Official Publications of the Soviet Union and Eastern Europe 1945-1980: A Selected Bibliography, ed. G. Walker, Mansell, London, 1982
Polish Research Guide, Polish Scientific Publishers, Warsaw, 1974
Who's Who in the Soviet Union, ed. Borys Lewytzskyi, Saur, Munich, 1984

10

Preparation for the Press

The research is done, the final draft completed, the length approximately right. (Some word-processor owners will have a built-in word-count facility, but those less fortunate must do it the hard way, taking an average number of words per page and multiplying by the number of pages – remembering to allow for any short pages and inserts – and rounding up the total to the nearest hundred words.)

If the great work is a novel or a play, all that remains is for the author either to print it out on his daisy wheel or letter-quality printer, or to type the fair copy himself electronically or manually, or – if he simply cannot face this task – to go to the expense of having it professionally typed. Those lucky enough to own word-processors or computers with word-processing programs will have made their final check on screen before printing out; everyone else should go through the typescript carefully once more before despatching it to literary agent or publisher.

The non-fiction book requires a little extra attention. The prelims must be written, the notes and references section and the bibliography (if any) compiled, some thought given to the provision of an index, although this will not actually be prepared until later. None of these chores, strictly speaking, comes within the province of 'research', but their importance as a whole in putting a professional finish on the typescript is such that they merit a brief mention here.

For the writer who needs to refresh his memory, the current *Writers' & Artists' Yearbook* carries short articles on the 'Preparation of Typescripts' and 'Correcting Proofs'. A useful series of pamphlet *Authors' and Printers' Guides*, published by Cambridge University Press and listed at the end of this chapter, will clarify the position further, but unfortunately some of these are now out of print; they are well worth snapping up if you come across them in a secondhand bookshop.

John Westwood's *Typing for Print* and Brenda Rowe's *Type It Yourself* are now also both out of print and not reprinting, but an excellent little handbook for the writer to keep at his elbow during this stage of his work is *The Typist's A-Z* by Edith Mackay. This useful publication deals with everything from punctuation, abbreviations and layout to the intricacies of square brackets; it also contains sections on the correction signs for typescripts, titles and forms of address, and the meaning of foreign words and phrases, among others.

Judith Butcher's *Copy-Editing*, on the other hand, is highly professional and directed more towards publishers' editors than to the layman; it too merits a place on the writer's bookshelf, however, since it gives many valuable hints for the final preparation of typescripts for the printer. Another standard work is the University of Chicago Press *A Manual of Style*. Finally, the latest issues of relevant British Standards are listed at the end of this chapter.

Prelims

These are the preliminary pages at the beginning of a book, known in the printing and publishing trade as 'prelims'. Normally they will consist of a title page, dedication, list of contents, list of illustrations, acknowledgments, abbreviations, preface or foreword. Not all of these will be required for every kind of book, and the publisher will have some say in the matter. It is up to the author to indicate, at this stage, what he intends to provide – i.e., if he wishes to include an 'Author's Note' or not. It will not matter if he cannot write the text of these as yet – it is quite sufficient to put a blank sheet in the typescript at the appropriate place or places, stating, for example, 'Acknowledgments' and below this, 'copy to follow'. The important thing is for the production manager and book designer to know that they are coming, so that they can allow for them in their calculations.

Notes and References

Consistency is the keyword here. If the book has been commissioned, the publisher may have sent the author a copy of the 'house style', or at least have stated a preference for the numbering and style of notes and references, such as whether they should appear at the foot of each page, after each chapter, or in a separate section at the end of the book. Failing such instruction, or if you do not yet have a publisher, it is advisable to study some published titles in a similar category of book and follow the same system.

Bibliography

Depending on whether the work is aimed at the popular or academic market, the bibliography may be selective or as comprehensive as you can make it. If the latter, it is usual to divide the entries into 'primary' and 'secondary' (or 'printed' and 'manuscript') sources, and to include not only books, but articles in periodicals and learned journals, as well as references to private papers consulted. Provided careful notes have been kept of all material used in the course of research, as suggested earlier in this handbook, the compilation of a bibliography should be quite straightforward. The normal arrangement of books and articles is in an alphabetical sequence, under the surname of the author. Care should be taken to list the particular editions used and to indicate any subsequent revised editions or reprints of each work, where possible.

The British Standard BS 1629, *Bibliographical references*, lays down recommendations for an internationally accepted set of rules for the guidance of those compiling bibliographies in books.

Preparation of the Typescript

The cardinal rules for typing material for publication stipulate that the text should be typed on one side of the paper only, in double spacing, with good margins (at least 1½ inches (4 cm) on the left hand side). Nowadays A4 size paper is preferable to the old quarto or foolscap, and it is helpful to the publisher if approximately the same number of lines are typed per page. Headings should be consistent throughout, and quoted matter of more than a few lines should be indented, without the use of quotation marks. Indent five spaces at the beginning of each paragraph, unless the publisher's house style asks for anything different. Start each chapter on a new page.

You do not need to be over-meticulous about the appearance of the typescript. There are bound to be a few additions, deletions or corrections when you come to re-read the text, and so long as these are absolutely legible and their place of insertion or deletion clear to the printer, it is unnecessary to go to the trouble of re-typing each amended page. Be very careful, however, about numbering pages: an insertion between pages 14 and 15, for example, would be numbered 14a, 14b and so one; but if page 15 is to be deleted altogether, the previous page should be numbered 14/15. Where an insertion does not take up the full page, always rule a line obliquely from left to right through the remaining part of the page to indicate that the text is continuous. It is far better to use white correcting fluid and to type

143

the correction in than to risk an erasure and handwritten alteration that may be ambiguous to the typesetter. (A few publishers producing small runs of specialized books require what is known as 'camera-ready' copy, typed on electronic machines with carbon ribbon, variable spacing and justified lines, which is then photographed and reproduced lithographically; here, each page must of course be perfect, although pure spelling mistakes and punctuation may be corrected – very carefully – with the aid of correction fluid.)

It is wise to make three copies of the final text, a top copy and two carbons; the publisher may ask for two, and the author should always retain one copy. If additional copies should be required later on, i.e. for an American or paperback publisher, photocopies can be made.

There are on the market special packs of carbonless typing paper that produce one top and one copy without the need for a carbon; the quality of the copy is consistent and good (essential for photocopying purposes), but the cost so high at present that they are to be recommended only for short typescripts such as poems, articles or short stories. On the other hand, good carbon film is expensive too, and the sheets should be renewed every 10 or 15 pages when typing a full-length book so as to achieve some uniformity. (The discarded carbons can be used again for less important copies, such as correspondence.)

Writers who are in the habit of leaving the final typing to the very last moment before their delivery deadline may find it useful to prepare in advance sets of paper (bond + bank paper interleaved with carbons to the number required); this can be done at any odd moment, while listening to the radio, for instance, or when suffering from 'writer's block'. The saving of time is remarkable.

Never staple pages together. Short stories or features may be fastened with paper clips, and so may individual chapters of a book; but a full-length typescript is best put into a ring binder or packed loose into a box. (Use the boxes in which reams of bond typing paper are sold).

Proof-correction

One of the last pre-publication chores facing the book author will be the correction of proofs, sometimes in both galley and page but, depending upon the type of book, often only in page. This will give him the opportunity to amend dates or statistics, to correct wrong spellings and any grave errors, but he must bear in mind that

Preparation for the Press

corrections exceeding a certain percentage (usually 10%) of the
original cost of setting are payable by the author; even the insertion
of a few commas can be quite costly. Printer's errors are not charged.

Sometimes, where a work of topical interest is involved and some
major event has taken place between the date of completion of the
manuscript and delivery of proofs, the publisher will find the space to
include a brief note to the effect that 'Since this book went to
press...' such and such has occurred, etc., but it cannot always be
counted on.

A list of signs used in proof correction will be found in the *Writers'
& Artists' Yearbook* and in the British Standard BS 5261, *Specification for typographic requirements, marks for copy preparation and
proof correction, proofing procedure*. Other valuable guides for
spelling, punctuation, division of words, and the use of capital and
lower case, are *Hart's Rules for Compositors and Readers* and the
Oxford Dictionary for Writers & Editors (which has replaced
Collins' Authors' & Printers' Dictionary).

The Index

Every non-fiction book merits a good index, and reviewers these
days are not only paying more attention than ever before to the
quality of indexing but are commenting unfavourably, where
appropriate, on the lack of indexes.

Most authors' contracts stipulate that the author shall provide the
index. It is however sometimes possible – and when, if ever, most
publishers have accepted the proposed Minimum Terms Agreement
negotiated by the Society of Authors and the Writers' Guild it may
hopefully become the norm – to get the publisher to agree to
contribute 50% of the cost, especially if a professional indexer is to
be employed. Some publishers have their own team of freelance
indexers on whom they can call; others seek recommendations from
the Society of Indexers, which was founded in 1957 to safeguard and
improve indexing standards and which maintains a register of
indexers suitably qualified in different subjects and types of
indexing. To assist those looking for an indexer for their work, the
Society now publishes annually a booklet entitled *Indexers Available*, which is distributed throughout the book trade; it lists practising
members' names, addresses, telephone numbers and their specialist
subjects.

There has long been controversy as to whether writers should or should not index their own books. Some people feel that an author is the ideal person, but others hold very strongly to the view that he may be too close to his own work to be able to produce a truly objective index. Certainly, as a general rule, it will almost always take him far longer than the expert. It is not generally realised that there is a great deal more to indexing than extracting the names of people and places and stringing them together in alphabetical order, so that when an author does decide to attempt it, he would be well advised to take the time and trouble to learn the basic rules.

Firstly, he must choose – and stick to – the form of alphabetical arrangement most suited to his book: either 'letter-by-letter' or 'word-by-word'. Then – and this is governed largely by space – he should give some thought to the layout and balance of the index and whether the sub-headings and sub-sub-headings (if any) will be indented or run on; both in layout and wording the sub-headings throughout must be consistent. There must be adequate cross-referencing of names and concepts, but not so much as to make the index unnecessarily long; care must be taken to avoid what is known as a 'wild goose chase', i.e. cross-references that never lead to the location of the subject matter in the text, as in, for example, 'Indexers, Society of, *see* Society of Indexers' and 'Society of Indexers, *see* Indexers, Society of'. The main function of an index is to direct the user quickly to the place or places in the text where he will find precisely the information he seeks.

Indexing is normally undertaken at page proof stage and, for this reason, it nearly always has to be done at speed in order to meet the printers' deadline. Here the micro-computer has really come into its own, and now that there is software available that has been specially designed to meet the professional indexer's needs, two of the most time-consuming stages of the job – the sorting of entries into the required order, and the printing out of the edited index copy – can be accomplished very quickly. But by no means all indexers are using computers as yet. Much manual indexing still goes on, the usual method being to mark on the page proofs (either with highlighter pen or by underlining) each name or concept to be indexed, and to write these on separate cards or slips which are filed alphabetically in a box as work proceeds; a certain amount of tightening up and editing of entries has to take place when all entries are assembled. In the course of his work the indexer may come across inconsistencies or inaccuracies that both the author and the publisher's editor have missed; these should be telephoned through to the editorial office immediately. A few printers will accept index copy on cards or slips, but it is preferable to type the index (double-spaced, allowing 32 characters per line) and to keep a carbon copy. The publisher will usually say that his tight production deadline will not permit him to send the indexer a proof for correction, but this should be insisted on wherever possible. Even the best printer can make a nonsense out of an index by failing to indent a sub-heading or by omitting or misprinting the occasional page reference – something that may not be spotted if the index is checked in the editorial office – and an index that is inaccurate is worse than no index at all.

These are but a few of the problems that confront the indexer. Authors interested in acquiring some basic training in indexing may take a correspondence course through the Rapid Results College, Tuition House, London SW19 4DS, and follow this with an advance course (also by correspondence) tutored by a Society of Indexers member. Among a number of excellent manuals on the subject are M. D. Anderson's *Book Indexing* (an admirable short introduction), the two 'standard' textbooks by Robert L. Collison, *Indexes and Indexing* and *Indexing Books*, and G. Norman Knight's *Indexing, The Art of*. British Standards BS 3700, *Recommendations for the preparation of indexes to books, periodicals and other publications*, and BS 1749, *Alphabetical arrangement and the filing order of numerals and symbols*, are the authoritative guides to current basic principles and practice. For further reading, the Society of Indexers' *Select Reading List on Indexing* (available to non-members) and also *Indexers on Indexing*, a selection of articles published in *The Indexer* between 1958 and 1968, are recommended. Hans Wellisch, President of the American Society of Indexers, has more recently published *Indexing and Abstracting*, the second volume of which is an international bibliography on the subject.

Names of suitably qualified indexers (general or specialist) may be obtained from the Registrar of the Society of Indexers, Mrs E. Wallis, 25 Leyborne Park, Kew Gardens, Surrey TW9 3HB (tel. 01-940 4771). For a copy of *Indexers Available*, together with other information about the Society, write to the Hon. Secretary, Mr D. T. O'Rourke, 38 Stanhope Road, Reading RG2 7HN.

A last word of advice

Once the proofs have been corrected and returned to the publisher, the author may safely return all borrowed books and documents to their respective libraries and/or owners. He may also wish to parcel up and store his original notes and early drafts. *It is important not to throw these away.* When eventually his book is published, there is always the possibility that it may arouse unexpected interest and may even lead to other related commissions; almost certainly he will receive a number of readers' letters either asking him to justify certain statements or to give further information. Some of these enquiries may come from researchers working in the same field. Bearing in mind the enormous help he himself has derived from the work of others, would it not be churlish and ungenerous to refuse or not to be in a position to pass on the fruits of his own research – especially any information gathered but not used – to other *bona fide* writers?

It should not be forgotten that all writers feed to a lesser or greater extent on the work of other writers. As the Californian playwright Wilson Mizner put is, 'When you steal from one author, it's plagiarism; if you steal from many, it's research'.

Authors' & Printers' Guides, Cambridge University Press
    titles in print:
    Book Design, by John Trevitt, 1980
    Book Indexing, by M. D. Anderson, 1971
    Copyright, by Christopher Scarles, 1980
    Typescripts, Proofs and Indexes, by Judith Butcher, 1980
    titles out of print:
    First Principles of Typography, by Stanley Morison, 1967
    Making an Index, by G. V. Carey, 1965
    Notes and References, by P. G. Burbidge, 1952
    Prelims and End-Pages, 2nd ed., by P. G. Burbidge, 1969
    Preparation of Manuscripts and Correction of Proofs, 6th ed., by
    B. Crutchley, 1970
    Punctuation, by G. V. Carey, 1957
British Standards (available from the British Standards Institution, 2
    Park Street, London W1A 2BS):

BS 1629 : 1976	*Recommendations for bibliographical references*
BS 1749 : 1985	*Alphabetical arrangement and the filing order of numerals and symbols*
BS 3700 : 1976 (reissued 1983)	*Recommendations for the preparation of indexes to books, periodicals and other publications*
BS 5261 : Part I : 1975	*Recommendations for the preparation of typescript copy for printing*
BS 5261 : Part II: 1976	*Specification for typographical requirements, marks for copy preparation and proof correction, proofing procedure*

BS 5271 C : 1976   *Marks for copy preparation and proof correction* (extract from BS 5261 : Part II) (currently under revision)

Copy-Editing, 2nd ed., by Judith Butcher, Cambridge University Press, Cambridge, 1981

Indexers on Indexing, ed. L. M. Harrod, Bowker, New York and London, 1978

Indexing and Abstracting: an international bibliography, 2 vols., by Hans Wellisch, ABC-Clio, 1980, 1985 (distributed in UK by Clio Press, Oxford)

Indexes and Indexing, 4th rev. ed., by R. L. Collison, Benn, London, and J. de Graff, New York, 1972

Indexing, Art of, by G. Norman Knight, Allen & Unwin, London, 1979

Indexing Books, by R. L. Collison, Benn, London, and J. de Graff, New York, 1969

Manual of Style, A, 13th ed., University of Chicago Press, Chicago and London, 1982

Oxford Dictionary for Writers and Editors, Oxford University Press, Oxford, 1981

Rules for Compositors and Readers at the University Press, 39th ed., (H. Hart), Oxford University Press, Oxford, 1983

Select List on Indexing, ed. Ann Hoffmann, Society of Indexers, London, 1978 (available to non-members from Mrs D. Frame, 26 Draycot Road, Wanstead, London E11 2NX, price £1.10 post free)

Type It Yourself, by Brenda Rowe, Penguin Books, Harmondsworth, 1981

Typist's A-Z, The, by Edith Mackay, Pitman Books, London, 1983

APPENDIX I

Selective List of Major Sources in the United Kingdom

This list is limited by space and should be used as a guideline only, in conjunction with the *Aslib Directory*, the HMSO booklet *Record Repositories in Great Britain* and other reference source guides mentioned in various sections of this handbook. Unless otherwise stated, the libraries and record offices are open to the public without formality. Addresses, telephone numbers and hours of opening are subject to change over the years, and while every effort has been made to bring information up to date at the time of going to press, intending visitors are advised to check in advance before travelling any distance and to reserve a seat.

The Copyright Libraries

British Library, Reference Division, Department of Printed Books, Great Russell Street, London WC1B 3DG (tel. 01-636 1544). Admission by reader's ticket. Mon., Fri., Sat., 9 – 5; Tues., Wed., Thurs., 9 – 9; closed for the week following the last complete week in October.

Bodleian Library, University of Oxford, Broad Street, Oxford OX1 3BG (tel. Oxford (0865) 244675). Admission by reader's ticket. Mon. – Fri., 9 – 10 (term), 9 – 7 (vacation); Sat., 9 – 1; closed last week in August.

Cambridge University Library, West Road, Cambridge CB3 9DR (tel. Cambridge (0223) 61441). Admission by reader's ticket. Mon. – Fri., 9 – 7; Sat., 9 – 1; closed for one week in September.

National Library of Scotland, George IV Bridge, Edinburgh EH1 1EW (tel. Edinburgh (031) 226 4531). Admission by reader's ticket. Mon. – Fri., 9.30 – 8.30; Sat., 9.30 – 1.

National Library of Wales, Aberystwyth, Dyfed SY23 3BU (tel. Aberystwyth (0970) 3816). Admission by reader's ticket. Mon. – Fri., 9.30 – 6; Sat., 9.30 – 5.

N.B. Trinity College Library, College Street, Dublin, in the Republic of Ireland, is also a copyright library. (Tel. Dublin (0001) 772 941).

Public Record Offices

Public Record Office, Ruskin Avenue, Kew, Richmond, Surrey TW9 4DU (tel. 01-876 3444) and Chancery Lane, London WC2A 1LR (tel. 01-405 0741). Admission by reader's ticket. Mon. – Fri., 9.30 – 5; closed for two weeks in October.

Scottish Record Office, H.M. General Register House, Edinburgh EH1 3YY (tel. Edinburgh (031) 556 6585). Admission by reader's ticket. Mon. – Fri., 9 – 4.45; Sat., 9 – 12.30 (Historical Search Room only).

Public Record Office of Northern Ireland, 66 Balmoral Avenue, Belfast BT9 6NY (tel. Belfast (0232) 661621/663286). Admission by reader's ticket. Mon. – Fri., 9.30 – 4.45; closed first two weeks in December.

General Register Offices

General Register Office (The Office of Population Censuses and Surveys): indexes to registers of births, marriages and deaths at St Catherine's House, 10 Kingsway, London WC2B 6JP (tel. 01-242 0262). Mon. – Fri., 8.30 – 4.30.

N.B. Census returns open for public inspection are at the Public Record Office building in Portugal Street, London WC2 (tel. 01-405 3488).

Principal Registry of the Family Division, Somerset House, Strand, London WC2R 1LP (tel. 01-405 7641, ext. 3097). Mon. – Fri., 10 – 4.30.

General Register Office for Scotland, New Register House, Edinburgh EH1 3YT (tel. Edinburgh (031) 556 3952). Mon. – Thurs., 9.30 – 4.30; Fri., 9.30 – 4.

General Register Office for Northern Ireland, Oxford House, 49 – 55 Chichester Street, Belfast BT1 4HL (tel. Belfast (0232) 35211). Mon. – Fri., 9.30 – 3.30.

N.B. The records for the whole of Ireland from 1864 to 1921 are at the office of the Registrar General, Custom House, Dublin, which houses the records of the Republic only since 1922.

Manuscript Collections/Registers of Archives

British Library Reference Division, Department of Manuscripts, Great Russell Street, London WC1B 3DG (tel. 01-636 1544). Admission to Student's Room by reader's ticket (applications at least 2 days in advance). Mon. – Sat., 10 – 4.45; closed first week in November.

N.B. The ordinary reader's ticket for the British Library does not admit to the Department of Manuscripts Students Room.

British Library Reference Division, Department of Oriental Printed Books and Manuscripts, Great Russell Street, London WC1B 3DG (tel. 01-636 1544). Admission by reader's ticket. Mon. – Fri., 9.30 – 4.45; Sat., 9.30 – 12.45; closed last week in October.

Royal Commission on Historical Manuscripts/National Register of Archives, Quality House, Quality Court, Chancery Lane, London WC2A 1HP (tel. 01-242 1198). Mon. – Fri., 9.30 – 5.

National Register of Archives (Scotland), West Register House, Charlotte Square, Edinburgh EH2 4DF (tel. Edinburgh (031) 556 6585). Mon. – Fri., 9 – 4.45.

Large collections of manuscripts are also housed at the Public Record Offices (see above) and at the various County Record Offices and University Libraries (see below).

County Record Offices/Regional Archives Centres

In this list opening times are not given for the individual offices: some are open all day throughout the working week, others close for lunch (or do not produce material during the lunch period), some are open late one evening in the week (but material must be ordered beforehand), others are shut either on Mondays or Saturdays. It is advisable to check prior to making a visit, as these opening hours are subject to change.

Avon

Bath City Record Office, Guildhall, Bath BA1 5AW (tel. 0225 61111, ext. 201)

Bristol Record Office, Council House, College Green, Bristol BS1 5TR (tel. 0272 266031, ext. 441/2)

Bedfordshire

Bedfordshire Record Office, County Hall, Bedford MK42 9AP (tel. 0234 63222, ext. 277)

Research for Writers

Berkshire

Berkshire Record Office, Shire Hall, Shinfield Park, Reading RG2 9XD (tel. 0734 875444, ext. 3182)

Buckinghamshire

Buckinghamshire Record Office, County Hall, Aylesbury HP20 1UA (tel. 0296 5000, ext. 588)

Cambridgeshire

Cambridge County Record Office, Shire Hall, Castle Hill, Cambridge CB3 0AP (tel. 0223 317281); also at Grammar School Walk, Huntingdon PE18 6LF (tel. 0480 52181, ext. 42)

Cheshire

Cheshire Record Office, The Castle, Chester CH1 2DN (tel. 0244 602574)
Chester City Record Office, Town Hall, Chester CH1 2HJ (tel. 0244 40144, ext. 2108)

Cleveland

Cleveland County Archives Department, 81 Borough Road, Middlesbrough TS1 3AA (tel. 0642 210944)

Cornwall

Cornwall County Record Office, County Hall, Truro TR1 3AY (tel. 0872 73698)
Royal Institution of Cornwall, County Museum, River Street, Truro TR1 2SJ (tel. 0872 72205)

Cumbria

Cumbria County Record Office, The Castle, Carlisle CA3 8UR (tel. 0228 23456, ext. 314/316; also at County Offices, Kendal LA9 4RQ (tel. 0539 21000) and at Duke Street, Barrow-in-Furness LA14 1XW (tel. 0229 31269)

Derbyshire

Derbyshire Record Office, County Offices, Matlock DE4 3AG (tel. 0629 3411, ext. 7347)

Devon

Devon Record Office, Castle Street, Exeter EX4 3PQ (tel. 0392 53509)

West Devon Record Office, Clare Place, Coxside, Plymouth PL4 0JW (tel. 0752 264685)

Dorset

Dorset Record Office, County Hall, Dorchester DT1 1XJ (tel. 0305 63131, ext. 4411)

Durham

Durham County Record Office, County Hall, Durham DH1 5UL (tel. 0385 64411, ext. 2474/2253)

Essex

Essex Record Office, County Hall, Chelmsford CM1 1LX (tel. 0245 267222, ext. 2104); and Central Library, Victoria Avenue, Southend-on-Sea SS2 6EX (tel. 0702 612621, ext. 49); Colchester and NE Essex Branch, Stanwell House, Stanwell Street, Colchester CO2 7DL (tel. 0206 572099)

Gloucestershire

Gloucestershire Record Office, Worcester Street, Gloucester GL1 3DW (tel. 0452 21444, ext. 227/8)

Hampshire

Hampshire Record Office, 20 Southgate Street, Winchester SO23 9EF (tel. 0962 63153)

Portsmouth City Records Office, 3 Museum Road, Portsmouth PO1 2LE (tel. 0705 829765)

Southampton City Record Office, Civic Centre, Southampton SO9 4XL (tel. 0703 23855, ext. 251)

Hereford and Worcester

Hereford and Worcester Record Office, Shirehall, Worcester WR1 1TR (tel. 0905 353366, ext. 3612)

Hereford Record Office, The Old Barracks, Harold Street, Hereford HR1 2QX (tel. 0432 65441)

St Helen's Record Office, Fish Street, Worcester WR1 2HN (tel. 0905 353366, ext. 3615/6)

Hertfordshire

Hertfordshire Record Office, County Hall, Hertford SG13 8DE (tel. 0992 54242)

Humberside

Humberside County Record Office, County Hall, Beverley, North Humberside HU17 9BA (tel. 0482 867131, ext. 3393/4)
South Humberside Area Record Office, Central Library, Town Hall Square, Grimsby DN31 1HX (tel. 0472 53481)
Kingston upon Hull City Record Office, 79 Lowgate, Kingston upon Hull HU1 2AA (tel. 0482 222015/6)

Kent

Kent County Archives Office, County Hall, Maidstone ME14 1XQ (tel. 0622 671411, ext. 4363) and at (SE Kent branch) Folkestone Central Library, Grace Hill, Folkestone CT20 1HD (tel. 0303 57583)

Lancashire

Lancashire Record Office, Bow Lane, Preston PR1 8ND (tel. 0772 54868, ext. 3039)

Leicestershire

Leicestershire Record Office, 57 New Walk, Leicester LE1 7JB (tel. 0533 554100, ext. 238)

Lincolnshire

Lincolnshire Archives Office, The Castle, Lincoln LN1 3AB (tel. 0522 25158)

London

Greater London Record Office, 40 Northampton Road, Clerken-well, London EC1R 0AB (tel. Archives, 01-633 6851; Library, 01-633 7132; Maps and Prints, 01-633 7193; Photographs, 01-633 3255). Closed last 2 weeks in October.
Due to be transferred to the Corporation of London on 1 April 1986.

Manchester

Greater Manchester Record Office, 56 Marshall Street, New Cross, Ancoats, Manchester M4 5FU (tel. 061-247 3383/3893)

Merseyside

Merseyside County Archives Service, RCA Building, 64-66 Islington, Liverpool L3 8LG (tel. 051-207 3697/8)
Liverpool Record Office, City Libraries, William Brown Street, Liverpool L3 8EW (tel. 051-207 2147, ext. 34)
Wirral Archives, Reference and Information Services, Birkenhead Central Library, Borough Road, Birkenhead L41 2XB (tel. 051-652 6106/7/8)

Midlands

Birmingham Reference Library, Central Library, Chamberlain Square, Birmingham B3 3HQ (tel. 021-235 4219)
Coventry City Record Office, Room 220, Broadgate House, Broadgate, Coventry CV1 1NG (tel. 0203 25555, ext. 2768)
Warwick University Modern Records Centre, The University Library, Coventry CV4 7AL (tel. 0203 24011, ext. 2014)

Norfolk

Norfolk Record Office, Central Library, Norwich NR2 1NJ (tel. 0603 611277, ext. 262)

Northamptonshire

Northamptonshire Record Office, Delapré Abbey, Northampton NN4 9AW (tel. 0604 62129)

Northumberland

Northumberland Record Office, Melton Park, North Gosforth, Newcastle-upon-Tyne NE3 5QX (tel. 0632 362680)

Nottinghamshire

Nottinghamshire Record Office, County House, High Pavement, Nottingham NG1 1HR (tel. 0602 54524)

Oxfordshire

Oxfordshire County Record Office, County Hall, New Road, Oxford OX1 1ND (tel. 0865 815203)

Shropshire

Shropshire Record Office, The Shirehall, Abbey Foregate, Shrewsbury SY2 6ND (tel. 0743 222406/7)

Somerset

Somerset Record Office, Obridge Road, Taunton TA2 7PU (tel. 0823 87600/78805)

Staffordshire

Staffordshire Record Office, County Buildings, Eastgate Street, **Stafford ST16 2LZ (tel. 0785 223121, ext. 7910)**
Lichfield Joint Record Office, Lichfield Library, Bird Street, Lichfield WS13 6PN (tel. 05432 56787)

Suffolk

Suffolk Record Office, Ipswich Branch, County Hall, St Helen's Street, Ipswich IP4 2JS (tel. 0473 55801, ext. 235)
Suffolk Record Office, Bury St Edmunds Branch, Schoolhall Street, Bury St Edmunds IP33 1RX (tel. 0284 63141, ext. 384)

Surrey

Surrey Record Office, County Hall, Penrhyn Road, Kingston-upon-Thames, KT1 2DN (tel. 01-546 1050, ext. 3561); Guildford Muniment Room, Castle Arch, Guildford GU1 3SX (tel. 0483 573942)

East Sussex

East Sussex Record Office, The Maltings, Castle Precincts, Lewes BN7 1YT (tel. 0273 475400)

West Sussex

West Sussex Record Office, West Street, Chichester PO19 1RN (tel. 0243 777100, ext. 2770/777983)

Tyne and Wear

Tyne and Wear Archives Department, Blandford House, West Blandford Street, Newcastle-upon-Tyne NE1 4JA (tel. 0632 326789); Local Studies Centre, Howard Street, North Shields NE30 1LY (tel. 0632 58211)

Warwickshire

Warwick County Record Office, Priory Park, Cape Road, Warwick CV34 4JS (tel. 0926 493431, ext. 2508)

Isle of Wight

Isle of Wight County Record Office, 26 Hillside, Newport PO30 2EB (tel. 0983 524031, ext. 132)

Wiltshire

Wiltshire County Record Office, County Hall, Trowbridge BA14 8JG (tel. 02214 3641, ext. 3500)

North Yorkshire

North Yorkshire County Record Office, County Hall, Northallerton DL7 8SG (tel. 0609 3123, ext. 455)
York City Archives, Exhibition Square, York YO1 2EW (tel. 0904 51533)

South Yorkshire

South Yorkshire County Record Office, Cultural Activities Centre, Ellin Street, Sheffield S1 4PL (tel. 0742 29191)
Doncaster Archives Department, King Edward Road, Balby, Doncaster DN4 0NA (tel. 0302 859811)
Sheffield City Libraries Archives Division, Central Library, Surrey Street, Sheffield S1 1XZ (tel. 0742 734756)

West Yorkshire

West Yorkshire Record Office, Registry of Deeds, Newstead Road, Wakefield WF1 2DE (tel. 0924 367111, ext. 2352)

Scotland

Argyll and Bute District Archives, Kilmory, Lochgilphead, Argyll PA31 8RT (tel. 0546 2177)
Central Regional Council Archives Department, Old High School, Spittal Street, Stirling FK8 1DG (tel. 0786 3111, ext. 466)
Dumfries and Galloway Regional Council Library Service (Archives), Ewart Public Library, Catherine Street, Dumfries DG1 1JB (tel. 0387 3820/2070)
Dundee District Archives and Records Centre, City Chambers, Dundee DD1 3BY (tel. 0382 23141, ext. 494)
Edinburgh District Archives, City Chambers, High Street, Edinburgh EH1 1YJ (tel. 031-225 2424, ext. 5196)
City of Glasgow Mitchell Library, 201 North Street, Glasgow G3 7DN (tel. 041-248 7030, ext. 139)

Grampian Regional Archives, Woodhill House, Ashgrove Road, West Aberdeen AB9 2LU (tel. 0224 682222, ext. 2130)

Orkney Archives Office, The Orkney Library, Laing Street, Kirkwall KW15 1NW (tel. 0856 3166, ext. 4)

Shetland Archives, 44 King Harald Street, Lerwick ZE1 0EQ (tel. 0595 3535, ext. 286)

Strathclyde Regional Archives, 30 John Street, Glasgow (tel. 041-221 9600, ext. 2021); all correspondence to P.O. Box 27, City Chambers, Glasgow G2 1DU

Wales

Clwyd Record Office, The Old Rectory, Hawarden, Deeside CH5 3NR (tel. 0244 532364) and 46 Clwyd Street, Ruthin LL15 1HP (tel. 08242 3077)

Dyfed Archives Service, County Hall, Carmarthen SA3 1JP (tel. 0267 233333, ext. 4182; Ceredigion Record Office, Swyddfa'r Sir, Marine Parade, Aberystwyth SY23 2DE (tel. 0970 617581, ext. 2120)

Glamorgan Archive Service, Mid Glamorgan County Hall, Cathays Park, Cardiff CF1 3NE (tel. 0222 28033, ext. 282)

Gwent County Record Office, County Hall, Cwmbran NP4 2XH (tel. 06333 67711)

Gwynedd Archives Service: Caernarfon Area Record Office, County Offices, Shirehall Street, Caernarfon LL55 1SH (tel. 0286 4121); Dolgellau Area Record Office, Cae Penarlag, Dolgellau LL40 2YB (tel. 0341 422341, ext. 261); Llangefni Area Record Office, Shire Hall, Llangefni LL77 7TW (tel. 0248 723262)

University Libraries (other than Oxford and Cambridge) with Important Manuscript Collections

Students, undergraduates and graduates of other universities are normally admitted without formality; temporary tickets will be issued to other *bona fide* researchers at the Librarian's discretion. At some libraries there are slightly amended opening hours during vacations. Please note that opening times and telephone extensions, where stated, are for the departments of manuscripts and archives. In all cases you should write in advance of your visit.

The main libraries of the University of Cambridge and the University of Oxford are listed under 'Copyright Libraries' above.

England

Birmingham University Library, P.O. Box 363, Birmingham B15 2TT (tel. 021-472 1301, ext. 2439). Mon. – Fri., 9 – 5. Closed Christmas and Easter vacations.

Durham University Library, Palace Green, Durham DH1 3RN (tel. 0385 61262). Mon. – Fri., 9 – 12.45, 2 – 4.45; Sat., 9 – 12 (not July/August)

Durham University Department of Palaeography and Diplomatic, 5, The College and The Prior's Kitchen, The College, Durham DH1 3EQ (tel. 0385 61478/64561). Mon. – Fri., 10 – 1, 2 – 5; Sat., 9.30 – 12.30 (term only)

Exeter University Library, Prince of Wales Road, Exeter EX4 4PT (tel. 0392 77911). Mon. – Fri., 9 – 5.30

Hull University, Brynmor Jones Library, Cottingham Road, Hull HU6 7RX (tel. 0482 46311). Mon. – Fri., 9 – 10 (term), 9 – 5.30 (vacation); Sat., 9 – 1

Keele University Library, Keele ST5 5BG (tel. 0782 621111, ext. 255). Mon. – Fri., 9.30 – 5, by appointment; Sat., by prior arrangement

Leeds University, Brotherton Library, Leeds LS2 9JT (tel. 0532 431751). Mon. – Fri., 9 – 5, by appointment

Liverpool University, Sydney Jones Library, P.O. Box 123, Liverpool L69 3DA (tel. 051-709 6022). Mon. – Fri., 9 – 5; Sat., by arrangement

University of London Library, Senate House, Malet Street, London WC1E 7HU (tel. 01-636 4514). Mon. – Fri., 9 – 5.30

John Rylands University Library of Manchester, Deansgate, Manchester M3 3EH (tel. 061-834 5343). Mon. – Fri., 9.30 – 5.30; Sat., 9.30 – 1, by appointment

Newcastle-upon-Tyne University Library, Queen Victoria Road, Newcastle-upon-Tyne NE1 7RU (tel. 0632 328511). Mon. – Fri., 9 – 5; Sat., 9 – 1, by written application

Nottingham University Library, University Park, Nottingham NG7 2RD (tel. 0602 56101). Mon. – Fri., 9 – 5, by appointment

Reading University Library, Whiteknights, Reading RG6 2AE (tel. 0734 84331, ext. 60). Mon. – Fri., 9 – 1, 2 – 5

Sheffield University Library, Western Bank, Sheffield S10 2TN (tel. 0742 78555, ext. 4328). Mon. – Thurs., 9 – 9.30, Fri., 9 – 5 (term); Mon. – Fri., 9 – 5 (vacation); Sat., 9 – 12.30

Southampton University Library, Southampton SO9 5NH (tel. 0703 559122, ext. 335). Mon. – Fri., 9 – 5

Sussex University Library, Falmer, Brighton BN1 9QL (tel. 0273 606755, ext. 884). Mon. – Fri., 9 – 5.30, by written application

Warwick University Library, Modern Records Centre, Coventry CV4 7AL (tel. 0203 24011). Mon. – Thurs., 9 – 1, 1.30 – 5; Fri., 9 – 1, 1.30 – 4

York University, Borthwick Institute of Historical Research, St Anthony's Hall, Peasholme Green, York YO1 2PW (tel. 0904 642315). Mon. – Fri., 9.30 – 1, 2 – 5, by appointment

Scotland

Aberdeen University Library, Manuscripts and Archives Section, King's College, Aberdeen AB9 2UB (tel. 0224 40241). Mon. – Fri., 9.15 – 4.30

Dundee University Library, Dundee DD1 4HN (tel. 0382 23181, ext. 245). Mon. – Fri., 9 – 5

Edinburgh University Library, 30 George Square, Edinburgh EH8 9LJ (tel. 031-667 1011, ext. 6628). Mon. – Fri., 9 – 5, by written application

Glasgow University Library, Department of Special Collections, Hillhead Street, Glasgow G12 8QE (tel. 041-334 2122). Mon. – Fri., 9 – 9.30, Sat., 9 – 12.30 (term); Mon. – Fri., 9 – 5, Sat., 9 – 12.30 (vacation)

St Andrews University Library, North Street, St Andrews KY16 9TR (tel. 0334 76161, ext. 514). Mon. – Fri., 9 – 12, 2 – 5, Sat. by arrangement

Wales

University College of North Wales Library, Department of Manuscripts, Bangor LL57 2DG (tel. 0248 51151, ext. 316). Mon., Tues., Thurs., 9.15 – 4.45, Wed., 9.15 – 8.50, Fri., 9.15 – 4.45 (term); Mon. – Fri., 9.15 – 4.45 (vacation)

Cathedral Archives and Libraries

Canterbury Cathedral Archives and Library, The Precincts, Canterbury, Kent CT1 2EG (tel. 0227 63510). Mon. – Fri., 9.30 – 12.45, 2 – 4.30, by appointment

Durham Dean and Chapter Library, The College, Durham DH1 3EH (tel. 0385 62489). Mon. – Fri., 9 – 1, 2.15 – 5. Closed in August

Exeter Cathedral Library and Archives, Bishop's Palace, Exeter EH1 1HX (tel. 0392 72894). Mon. – Fri., 2 – 5

Salisbury Cathedral Chapter Archives, The Close, Salisbury SP1 2EL (tel. 0722 22519). Mon. − Fri., 10 − 12.30, 2.15 − 4, by appointment

York Minster Library, Dean's Park, York YO1 2JD (tel. 0904 25308). Mon. − Fri., 9 − 5, by appointment

Westminster Abbey Muniment Room and Library, London SW1P 3PA (tel. 01-222 5152). Mon. − Fri., 10 − 1, 2 − 4.45, application in writing necessary

Westminster Diocesan Archives (Roman Catholic), Archbishop's House, Ambrosden Avenue, London SW1P 1QJ (tel. 01-834 1964). Mon. − Fri., 10 − 5, by appointment

Winchester Cathedral Library, The Close, Winchester SO23 9LS (tel. 0962 68580). Opening days and times subject to alteration; written application necessary

Other Major Reference Libraries

Belfast: Irish and Local Studies Department, Central Library, Royal Avenue, Belfast BT1 1EA (tel. 0232 43233)

Birmingham Reference Library, Central Library, Chamberlain Square, Birmingham B3 3HQ (tel. 021-235 4511)

Cardiff: Central Reference Library, The Hayes, Cardiff CF1 2QU (tel. 0222 382116)

Edinburgh: Central Library, George IV Bridge, Edinburgh EH1 1EG (tel. 031-225 5584)

Glasgow: Mitchell Library, North Street, Glasgow G3 7DN (tel. 041-221 7030)

Liverpool: Brown, Picton and Hornby Libraries, William Brown Street, Liverpool L3 8EW (tel. 051-207 2147)

London: Westminster Central Reference Library, St Martin's Street, London WC2H 7HP (tel. 01-798 2034/2036)

Manchester: Central Library, St Peter's Square, Manchester M2 5PD (tel. 061-236 9422)

Private Subscription Libraries

London Library, 14 St James's Square, London SW1Y 4LG (tel. 01-930 7705). Mon. − Sat., 9.30 − 5.30; late evening Thurs. to 7.30. £70 per year

Highgate Literary and Scientific Library, 11 South Grove, Highgate Village, London N6 6BS (tel. 01-340 3343). Mon. Tues., Thurs., Fri., 10 – 1, 3 – 6; Wed., Sat., 10 – 1. £12 per year (£18 family subscription)

Space does not permit the listing of private subscription libraries in the provinces, but these will be well-known to readers living locally; or consult the yellow pages of the local telephone directories.

Short List of Subjects and Sources

Advertising

Advertising Association Library, Abford House, 15 Wilton Road, London SW1V 1NJ (tel. 01-828 2771). Mon. – Fri., 10 – 1, 2 – 5. Open to public for reference, but only members may borrow books.

Agriculture

Institute of Agricultural History and Museum of English Rural Life, University of Reading, Whiteknights, Reading RG6 2AG (tel. 0734 875123, ext. 475). Mon. – Fri., 9.30 – 1, 2 – 5, by appointment.

Air Force

Royal Air Force Museum, Department of Aviation Records, Aerodrome Road, Hendon, London NW9 5LL (tel. 01-205 2266). Mon. – Fri., 10 – 4.30, by appointment only.

See also under 'World Wars I and II'

Architecture

British Architectural Library, Royal Institute of British Architects, 66 Portland Place, London W1N 4AD (tel. 01-580 5533). Mon., 10 – 5; Tues. – Thurs., 10 – 8; Fri., 10 – 7; Sat., 10 – 1.30. Closed in August.

Art

British Museum, Department of Prints and Drawings, Great Russell Street, London WC1B 3DG (tel. 01-636 1544). Admission by ticket (apply in advance). Mon. – Fri., 10 – 1, 2.15 – 4; Sat., 10 – 12.30.

Courtauld Institute of Art Library, 20 Portman Square, London
W1H 0BE (tel. 01-935 9292). Mon. – Fri., 10 – 7 (term); 10 – 6
(vacation). Closed in August. Outside researchers by arrangement. Will be moving *c.* 1987 to the North Block, Somerset House
Fine Arts Library (incorporating the Preston Blake Library), Central
Reference Library, 2nd floor, St Martin's Street, London WC2H
7HP (tel. 01-798 2038). Mon. – Fri., 10 – 7; Sat., 10 – 5.
Victoria & Albert Museum Library, Cromwell Road, London SW7
2RL (tel. 01-589 6371). Mon. – Thurs., 10 – 1, 2 – 5; Sat., 10 – 1;
closed on Fridays. N.B. A specially endorsed reader's ticket is
required for access to certain MSS and reserved material in the
National Art Library.

Banking and Commerce

Bank of England Information Division, Threadneedle Street, London EC2R 8AH (tel. 01-601 4411). Telephone or written
enquiries only. The Bank of England and other major banks will
grant access to historical records only when applications are
supported by a university or other centre of research.
Central Reference Library, Ground Floor, St Martin's Street,
London WC2H 7HP (tel. 01-798 2034). Mon. – Fri., 10 – 7; Sat.,
10 – 5.

Births, Marriages and Deaths

See under 'General Register Offices' (above) and 'Genealogy' in this
list.

Broadcasting

BBC Data Enquiry Service, Room 3, The Langham, Portland Place,
London W1A 1AA (tel. 01-927 5600/4338). Written or telephone
enquiries only. Fees on request.
BBC Written Archives Centre, Caversham Park, Reading RG4 8TZ
(tel. 0734 472742, ext. 281/282). Tues. – Fri. 9.45 – 1, 2 – 5.15,
by appointment only. Postal research queries undertaken by staff;
fees on request.

Business

British Library Business Information Service, Science Reference
Library, 25 Southampton Buildings, Chancery Lane, London
WC2A 1AW (tel. 01-404 0406). Mon. – Fri., 9.30 – 9; Sat.,
10 – 1.

Research for Writers

Business Archives Council, Denmark House, 15 Tooley Street, London SE1 2PN (tel. 01-407 6110). Will assist in tracing records of commercial and industrial undertakings.
City Business Library, Gillett House, 55 Basinghall Street, London EC2V 5BX (tel. 01-638 0215). Mon. – Fri., 9.30 – 5.30.
Companies House (Department of Trade and Industry), 55-71 City Road, London EC1Y 1BB (tel. 01-253 9393) and Companies Registration Office, Crown Way, Maindy, Cardiff CF4 3UZ (tel. 0222 45915). Mon. – Fri., 9.30 – 3.45. Microfilm copies of company records in London, files in Cardiff.

Census Returns

Public Record Office, Land Registry Building, Portugal Street entrance, London WC2A 3PH (tel. 01-405 3488). Admission by reader's ticket. Mon. – Fri., 9.30 – 5.

Costume

The Costume Society: enquiries to Hon. Secretary, Nigel Arch, at Court Dress Collection, Kensington Palace, London W8 4PX (tel. 01-937 9561).

Films

National Film Archive, British Film Institute, 81 Dean Street, London W1V 6AA (tel. 01-437 4355). Reference facilities only to non-members. Mon. – Fri., 10 – 5.30.
N.B. The book library and information service of the Institute is at 127 Charing Cross Road, London WC2 (tel. no. as for the Archive). Tues., Wed., 11 – 9; Thurs., Fri., 11 – 6; closed Mondays and Saturdays.

Genealogy and Heraldry

College of Arms, Queen Victoria Street, London EC4 4BT (tel. 01-248 2762). Mon. – Fri., 10 – 4; Sat. by appointment.
N.B. There are no public search rooms. Research is undertaken only by the Heralds and their staff, on a fee-paying basis.
Institute of Heraldic and Genealogical Studies Library, 79-82 Northgate, Canterbury, Kent CT1 1BA (tel. 0227 68664). Mon., Wed., Fri., 10 – 5, by appointment. Non-members pay a fee (currently £3.00 per half day, £5.00 per full day).
London Regional Genealogical Library of the Church of Jesus Christ of Latter-Day Saints (of Salt Lake City, Utah, USA), 64-68 Exhibition Road, London SW7 2PA (tel. 01-589 8561). Mon. – Fri., 9 – 9; Sat., 9 – 1.

Religious Society of Friends, Friends House, Euston Road, London NW1 2BJ (tel. 01-387 3601). Mon. – Fri., 10 – 5; closed for one week in August (variable from year to year). *Bona fide* researchers providing suitable introductions/letters of recommendation may use the Library on payment of a search fee (currently £2 per hour); proxy searches (carried out by staff), £8 per hour.

Society of Genealogists Library, 14 Charterhouse Buildings, Goswell Road, London EC1M 7BA (tel. 01-251 8799). Tues., Fri., Sat., 10 – 6; Wed., Thurs., 10 – 8; closed on Mondays. Non-members pay search fees (currently £2.00 for one hour; £5.00 for half day (3½ hours); £7.50 for full day). Closed for one week in February and one week in October.

Geography and Maps

British Library Reference Division, Department of Printed Books, Map Library, British Museum (King Edward Building), London WC1B 3DG (tel. 01-636 1544). Admission by reader's ticket. Mon. – Sat., 9.30 – 4.30; closed for the week following the last complete week in October.

Royal Geographical Society, Kensington Gore, London SW7 2AR (tel. 01-589 5466). Mon. – Fri., 10 – 5. Library open to *bona fide* researchers by arrangement; map room open to general public.

Government and Official Information

British Library Reference Division, Department of Printed Books, Official Publications Library, Great Russell Street, London WC1B 3DG (tel. 01-636 1544, ext. 234/235). Admission by reader's ticket. Mon., Fri., Sat., 9.30 – 4.45; Tues., Wed., Thurs., 9.30 – 8.45; closed for the week following the last complete week in October.

Central Office of Information, Hercules Road, Westminster Bridge Road, London SE1 7DU (tel. 01-928 2345). Telephone or written enquiries only.

India Office Library and Records, 197 Blackfriars Road, London SE1 8NG (tel. 01-928 9531). Mon. – Fri., 9.30 – 5.45; Sat., 9.30 – 12.45. Newspaper reading room at Bush House, Aldwych, London WC2B 4PH, Tues., Thurs. 10 – 5.30 only.

Public Record Office, Ruskin Avenue, Kew, Richmond, Surrey TW9 4DU (tel. 01-876 3444) and Chancery Lane, London WC2A 1LR (tel. 01-405 0741). Admission by reader's ticket. Mon. – Fri., 9.30 – 5; closed for two weeks in October.

See also under 'Parliament'.

Law

Inner Temple Library, Inner Temple, London EC4Y 7DA (tel.
01-353 2959). Mon. – Fri., 10 – 1. Written application necessary.

Lincoln's Inn Library, Lincoln's Inn, London WC2A 3TN (tel.
01-242 4371). Mon. – Fri., 9.30 – 7.

Middle Temple Library, Middle Temple Lane, London EC4Y 9BT
(tel. 01-353 4303). Mon. – Fri., 9.30 – 7; closes earlier on certain
days.

N.B. Use of these libraries is limited to members of the legal profession. For other law libraries, see the *Aslib Directory*.

London

Corporation of London Records Office, Guildhall, London EC2P
2EJ (tel. 01-606 3030, ext. 2251). Mon. – Fri., 9.30 – 5; Sat., by
arrangement.

Greater London Record Office, 40 Northampton Road, Clerken-
well, London EC1R 0AB; (tel. Archives, 01-633 6851; Library,
01-633 7132; Maps & Prints, 01-633 7193; Photographs,
01-633 3255). Tues. – Fri., 10 – 4.45; late night Tues., to 7; closed
last two weeks in October.

N.B. The Record Office is due to be transferred to the Corporation
of London on 1 April 1986.

Guildhall Library, Aldermanbury, London EC2P 2EJ (tel. 01-606
3030). Mon. – Sat., 9.30 – 5.

Westminster City Libraries, Westminster History Collection,
158-160 Buckingham Palace Road, London SW1W 9UD (tel.
01-798 2180). Mon. – Fri., 9.30 – 7; Sat., 9.30 – 5.

N.B. A number of London borough public libraries hold sizeable
local history collections. Consult current edition of *Record Repositories in Great Britain*, HMSO, London.

Medicine

Lewis's Medical, Scientific and Technical Lending Library, 136
Gower Street, London WC1E 6BS (tel. 01-387 4282). Postal and
non-postal subscription rates, according to number of volumes
borrowed. Mon. – Fri., 9 – 5; Sat., 9 – 1.

Marylebone Public Library Medical Library (Westminster City
Libraries), Marylebone Road, London NW1 5PS (tel. 01-798
1039). Mon. – Fri., 9.30 – 7; Sat., 9.30 – 5. Reference and lending
facilities (tickets from other public libraries may be used).

Royal College of Physicians of London Library, 11 St Andrew's
Place, London NW1 4LE (tel. 01-935 1174). Mon. – Fri., 10 – 5.
Bona Fide researchers not members of the profession may use the
reference facilities only.

Royal College of Surgeons of England Library, 35-43 Lincoln's Inn
Fields, London WC2A 3PN (tel. 01-405 3474). Admission by
introduction from a graduate of the College. Mon. – Fri., 10 – 6.
Closed in August.
Wellcome Institute for the History of Medicine Library, The
Wellcome Building, 183 Euston Road, London NW1 2BP (tel.
01-387 4477). Mon. – Fri., 9.45 – 5.15.
For further information see the latest edition of *Directory of Medical
Libraries in the British Isles*, Library Association, London.

Military

Liddell Hart Centre for Military Archives, King's College, Strand,
London WC2R 2LS (tel. 01-836 5454, ext. 2187). Mon. – Fri.,
9.30 – 5.30 (term); 9.30 – 4.30 (vacation), by written application.
N.B. 20th century records only.
Ministry of Defence Library, Old War Office Building, Whitehall,
London SW1A 2EU (tel. 01-218 0015). Telephone or written
enquiries only.
National Army Museum, Royal Hospital Road, London SW3 4HT
(tel. 01-730 0717). Admission by reader's ticket. Tues. – Sat.,
10 – 4.30. Now handles research enquiries for Society for Army
Historical Research.
Public Record Office, Ruskin Avenue, Kew, Richmond, Surrey TW9
4DU (tel. 01-876 3444) and Chancery Lane, London WC2A 1LR
(tel. 01-405 0741). Admission by reader's ticket. Mon. – Fri.,
9.30 – 5; closed for two weeks in October.
See also under 'World Wars I and II'

Music

British Library Reference Division, Department of Printed Books,
Music Library, Great Russell Street, London WC1B 3DG (tel.
01-636 1544). Printed music and books are applied for and seen
in the Music Reading Area of the Official Publications Library,
manuscript music in the Students' Room of the Department of
Manuscripts. Hours of opening as for Official Publications
Library, Department of Manuscripts, see under 'Government and
Official Information' and 'Manuscript Collections' above.
Royal College of Music Reference Library, Prince Consort Road,
London SW7 2BS (tel. 01-589 3643). Admission by reader's
ticket. Mon. – Fri., 10 – 5; closed late July to early September, also
for two weeks at Christmas and at Easter.

Research for Writers

Royal Opera House Archives, Covent Garden, London WC2E 7QA (tel. 01-240 1200, ext. 235). Mon. – Fri., 10 – 1, 2 – 6. *Bona fide* researchers, on written application.

Natural History

British Museum (Natural History) Library, Cromwell Road, London SW7 5BD (tel. 01-589 6323). Mon. – Fri., 10 – 4.30.

Royal Botanic Gardens Library and Archives, Kew, Richmond, Surrey, TW9 3AE (tel. 01-940 1171). Mon. – Thurs., 9 – 4.30; Fri., 9 – 5. Prior application to consult the archives is necessary.

Naval

National Maritime Museum Library, Romney Road, Greenwich, London SE10 9NF (tel. 01-858 4422). Tues. – Fri., 10 – 4 (Mondays open to reader's ticket holders only).

Newspapers and periodicals

British Library Newspaper Library, Colindale Avenue, London NW9 5HE (tel. 01-200 5515). Admission by reader's ticket. Mon. – Sat., 10 – 5; closed for the week following the last complete week in October.

British Library Reference Division, Department of Printed Books, Great Russell Street, London WC1B 3DG (tel. 01-636 1544), for periodicals (monthly or quarterly), to be seen in the main Reading Room or North Library Gallery. Mon., Fri., Sat., 9 – 5; Tues., Wed., Thurs., 9 – 9; closed for the week following the last complete week in October.

Parliament

House of Lords Record Office, House of Lords, Palace of Westminster, London SW1A 0AA (tel. 01-219 3074). Mon. – Fri., 9.30 – 5.30. Intending searchers should write to the Clerk of the Records in advance, giving at least one week's notice and details of the nature of their research and/or specific documents they wish to consult.

See also under 'Government and Official Information'

Politics (20th century)

British Library of Political and Economic Science (London School of Economics), 10 Portugal Street, London WC2A 2HD (tel. 01-405 7686), by appointment.

Churchill College Archives Centre, Churchill College, Cambridge CB3 0DS (tel. 0223 61200, ext. 378). Mon. – Fri., 9.30 – 12.30, 1.30 – 5, by appointment with the Archivist. N.B. Certain collections are subject to special conditions of access.

Recorded Sound

National Sound Archive, 29 Exhibition Road, London SW7 2AS (tel. 01-589 6603). Mon. – Fri., 10.30 – 5.30, with late opening Thurs., to 9, preferably by appointment.

Religion

Catholic Central Library, 47 Francis Street, London SW1P 1QR (tel. 01-834 6128). Non-members for reference and research only. Mon. – Fri., 10.30 – 6.30; Sat., 10.30 – 4.30

Church House Record Centre, Dean's Yard, London SW1P 3NZ (tel. 01-222 9011). Mon. – Fri., 10 – 5, by appointment.

Dr Williams's Library, 14 Gordon Square, London WC1H 0AG (tel. 01-387 3727). Mon., Wed., Fri., 10 – 5; Tues., Thurs., 10 – 6; closed first half of August. Admission by recommendation; subscription rate for borrowers (details on application to Librarian).

Jewish Museum and Central Library, Woburn House, Upper Woburn Place, London WC1H 0EP (tel. 01-387 3081). Write to the Curator for information.

Lambeth Palace Library, London SE1 7JU (tel. 01-928 6222). *Bona fide* students, others by special permission. Mon. – Fri., 10 – 5. Closed for ten days at Christmas and at Easter.

Methodist Archives and Research Centre, formerly at Epworth House, London, are now housed at the John Rylands University Library of Manchester, Deansgate, Manchester M3 3EH (tel. 061-834 5343). Mon. – Fri., 9.30 – 5.30; Sat., 9.30 – 1.

Sion College, Victoria Embankment, London EC4Y 0DN (tel. 01-353 7983). Mon. – Fri., 10 – 5. Annual subscription rates and temporary membership available.

See also under 'Cathedral Archives and Libraries'

Royal Archives

By special permission of the Keeper of the Queen's Archives, Windsor Castle, Berks. Apply in writing.

Science and Technology

Central Reference Library, Ground Floor, St Martin's Street, London WC2H 7HP (tel. 01-798 2034). Mon. – Fri., 10 – 7; Sat., 10 – 5.

Imperial College of Science and Technology Archives, Sherfield Building, Imperial College, London SW7 2AZ (tel. 01-589 5111, ext. 2039/2096). Mon. – Fri., 10 – 5.30, by appointment.

Royal Society of London Library, 6 Carlton House Terrace, London SW1Y 5AG (tel. 01-839 5561). Mon. – Fri., 10 – 5. Admission on introduction by a Fellow: *bona fide* researchers on written application.

Science Museum Library, Exhibition Road, London SW7 5NH (tel. 01-589 3456). Mon. – Fri., 10 – 5.30.

Science Reference Library (British Library Reference Division): Holborn Reading Room, 25 Southampton Buildings, Chancery Lane, London WC2A 1AW (tel. 01-405 8721, ext. 3344/5) (inventive sciences, engineering, industrial technologies and commerce); Aldwych Reading Room, 9 Kean Street, Drury Lane, London WC2B 4AT (tel. 01-323 7288, ext. 229) (life sciences and technologies, medicine, biotechnology, earth sciences, astronomy and pure mathematics); Foreign Patents Reading Room, Chancery House, Southampton Buildings, Chancery Lane, London WC2 (tel. 01-405 8721, ext. 3411). Opening hours: Holborn, Mon. – Fri., 9.30 – 9; Sat., 10 – 1. Aldwych, Mon. – Fri., 9.30 – 5.30. Chancery House, Mon. – Fri., 9.30 – 5.30.

See also Lewis's Lending Library, listed under 'Medicine'

Theatre

The British Theatre Museum, formerly at Leighton House, and the Enthoven Collection, formerly at the Victoria & Albert Museum have now been combined and will be reopening as The Theatre Museum in Covent Garden, probably by 1987; meanwhile the collections are closed to the public.

Mander and Mitchenson Theatre Collection, 5 Venner Road, Sydenham, London SE26 5EQ (tel. 01-778 6730). Open to *bona fide* researchers by appointment. Will be moving, probably during 1986/7, to The Mansion, Beckenham Place Park, Beckenham, Kent (tel. 01-658 7725).

Society for Theatre Research: collection at University of London Library, Senate House, Malet Street, London WC1E 7HU (tel. 01-636 4514). Write to Joint Hon. Secretaries for information.

N.B. During closure of the main collections above-mentioned, researchers may find information in the following publications:

A Directory of Theatre Research, ed. Diana Howard, Society for Theatre Research/Library Association RSIS, due for publication late 1985.

The London Stage, a series published by Scarecrow, Metuchen, N.J., USA, consisting of a day-by-day calendar of plays produced at the major London theatres; 9 vols to date, covering the period 1890-1929, with indexes.

Transport

Institute of Transport Library, 80 Portland Place, London W1N 4DP (tel. 01-636 9952). *Bona fide* researchers may use the reference facilities. Mon. – Fri., 10 – 5.

United Nations

United Nations Information Centre Library, Ship House, 20 Buckingham Gate, London SW1 (tel. 01-630 1981). Mon., Wed., Thurs., 10 – 1, 2 – 5.

Weather

National Meteorological Library, London Road, Bracknell, Berks RG12 2SZ (tel. 0344 20242). *Bona fide* researchers admitted, preferably by appointment; otherwise written enquiries. Mon. – Thurs., 9 – 5; Fri., 9 – 4.30.

Wills

Borthwick Institute of Historical Research, St Anthony's Hall, Peaseholme Green, York YO1 2PW (tel. 0904 642315). Mon. – Fri., 9.30 – 1, 2 – 5, by appointment; closed for two weeks in late August. (P.C.Y. Wills).

Principal Registry of the Family Division, Somerset House, Strand, London WC2R 1LP (tel. 01-405 7641). Mon. – Fri., 10 – 4.30. (Wills and Administrations since 1858).

Public Record Office, Chancery Lane, London, WC2A 1LR (tel. 01-405 0741). Admission by reader's ticket. Mon. – Fri., 9.30 – 5; closed for two weeks in October. (P.C.C. Wills).

World Wars I and II

Churchill College Archives Centre, Cambridge CB3 0DS (tel. 0223 61200, ext. 378). Mon. – Fri., 9 – 12.30, 1.30 – 5, by appointment with the Archivist. (Papers of military and naval commanders, politicians and scientists; certain collections subject to special conditions of access).

Imperial War Museum Library, Lambeth Road, London SE1 6HZ
(tel. 01-735 8922). Mon. – Fri., 10 – 5, preferably by
appointment. Closed last two full weeks in October.

Wiener Library, Institute of Contemporary History, 4 Devonshire
Street, London W1N 2BH (tel. 01-636 7247/8). Research fee
payable for extensive use, but short-term use of reference facilities
free. Mon. – Fri., 10 – 5.30. N.B. The collection of books was
mostly transferred to Tel Aviv University in 1980, but the bulk of
the material has been retained on microfilm in London.

APPENDIX II

Reference Books for the Writer

Good reference books are expensive, and the average writer cannot afford to compete with a library in keeping his personal collection fully up to date. He would be foolish even to try. What he buys, therefore, must be related to his own pocket, mobility and access to a well-stocked reference library, as well as to the special nature of his work.

Some basic suggestions for a writer's bookshelf are listed below. It is recommended that a plan for systematic renewal should be worked out, whereby you replace the essential yearbooks annually and other books in rotation. Those which are discarded may be sold to a secondhand book-dealer and the proceeds put towards the purchase of new editions. Excellent reference works may often be picked up in secondhand bookshops for a fraction of their original cost and are a good buy for those not engaged on highly topical work; the information they contain can be supplemented or updated by the occasional visit to the library or, in case of urgent need, by a telephone call to the reference librarian. Remainder dealers also frequently sell reference books at substantial discounts, and you should also keep an eye open for special offers advertised by book clubs. Paperbacks are by no means to be scorned: although naturally they will not stand up to as much handling as hard-covers, you will not be so reluctant to discard them when revised editions become available – nor, in the meantime, will you feel guilty about giving them the full 'working tool' treatment, annotating and marking them as your research proceeds.

At the end of a major project you may decide to dispose of a number of books in order to create shelf space for a new set related to your next work, and here again the secondhand bookseller with whom you are in the habit of dealing will undoubtedly give you a fair price. Depending on shelf space, do not however be *too* ruthless! (How to locate specialist booksellers will be found on page 30, and details of bookfinding services on page 37).

Suggested Basic Reference Library for the Writer

The essential items are:

1 A good English dictionary.

   The *Oxford English Dictionary*, published in 13 volumes, 1884-1928, with three supplements to date, is the most detailed (a compact edition, with reading glass, was brought out in 1971); but for most writers' purposes The *Shorter Oxford English Dictionary* 2 vols, 3rd ed. with revised addenda, 1973, compiled on historical principles, will be perfectly adequate. *Webster's Third New International Dictionary of the English Language*, 2 vols, 1976, concentrates on current usage, but is expensive (standard edition, £110; de luxe edition, £130). *Collins Dictionary of the English Language*, first published in 1979, and *Chambers Twentieth Century Dictionary*, 4th ed., 1983, are excellent single-volume, up-to-date dictionaries. For those who like to keep a smaller dictionary handy for quick reference, the *Concise Oxford Dictionary*, 7th ed., 1982, the *Oxford Paperback Dictionary*, 2nd ed., 1985 or the *Penguin English Dictionary* are ideal. Already mentioned in chapter 10, a recommended addition would be the *Oxford Dictionary for Writers and Editors*, 1981.

2 A good atlas, plus, if possible, a world gazetteer.

   '*The Times' Atlas of the World*, rev. ed., 1985, is one of the best (currently £55.00), or there is '*The Times' Concise Atlas of the World*, rev. ed., 1985, at £18.50. *The Hamlyn Reference Atlas of the World*, 1985, is right up to date, while *Webster's New Geographical Dictionary*, 1976, contains over 47,000 place names and a great deal of useful data. *The Statesman's Year Book World Gazetteer*, by John Paxton, Macmillan, London, 2nd ed., 1979, is the best of its kind.

   N.B. Atlases are brought up to date every few years, and it is wise to buy the latest edition of the best you can afford. Bowker publish a useful *International Maps and Atlases in Print*, edited by Kenneth L. Winch, 2nd ed., 1976, but as this is now rather out of date, and unlikely to be revised, the advice of a reputable firm such as Stanfords International Map Centre, 12-14 Long Acre, London WC2E 9LP (tel. 01-836 1321) should be sought before making a major purchase.

3 A road atlas/gazetteer of the British Isles.

   The Ordnance Survey Atlas of Great Britain, 1982, the *Bartholomew Gazetteer of Britain* and the *AA Great Britain Road Atlas* are all excellent.

4 An encyclopedia.
Chambers' Encyclopaedia, Encyclopaedia Britannica, Everyman's Encyclopaedia and the *Macmillan Family Encyclopedia* are all to be recommended, and the choice will depend on how much money you have to spend. Obviously you should choose the most up-to-date at the time of purchase, but so far as the *Britannica* is concerned, if at any time you have the opportunity to acquire a secondhand set of the 9th (the so-called 'scholars') edition, or the 11th (the most extensive and the last to be published in the UK), with its later supplements, you would be well advised to snap them up. The recent 15th edition, 32 volumes, 1974, known also as *Britannica 3*, is quite differently arranged. *Everyman's Encyclopaedia*, 6th edition, 1978, is an entirely updated and re-set edition, very good value at £195. The *Macmillan Family Encyclopedia*, new edition, 21 volumes, 1985, tends rather more to the 'popular' than to the 'academic' in content, but it is well illustrated and fully up to date. Among the single-volume works that are so valuable for quick reference are the *Macmillan Encyclopedia*, 3rd edition, 1985, and the *Hamlyn Modern World Encyclopedia*, 1980, reprinted 1984.

5 *Roget's Thesaurus of English Words and Phrases*. A revised edition was published by Longman in 1982 and is available in a standard or de luxe edition. There is also a Penguin paperback edition. Also useful is *Roget's International Thesaurus: the Complete Book of Synonyms and Antonyms in American and British Usage*, 3rd edition, Crowell, New York, 1962.

6 *Fowler's Modern English Usage*, 2nd edition, revised by Sir E. Gowers, Oxford University Press, 1965. This can be purchased in paperback as a boxed set together with the *Oxford Paperback Dictionary*.

7 *Brewer's Dictionary of Phrase and Fable*, 13th edition, revised, Cassell, London, 1981.

8 A good dictionary of quotations (or more than one).
The Oxford Dictionary of Quotations, 3rd edition, Oxford University Press, 1980, and *Bartlett's Familiar Quotations*, 16th edition, revised and enlarged by E. M. Beck, Macmillan, London, 1985, are standard works. *The International Thesaurus of Quotations*, compiled by Rhoda T. Tripp, Allen & Unwin, London, 1975, covers a wider field; it is also available as a Penguin paperback. Other useful volumes include *Quotations in History: A Dictionary of Historical Quotations, c.800* A.D. *to the Present*, compiled by A. and V. Palmer, Harvester Press, 1976, the *Dictionary of Foreign Quotations*, compiled by R. Collison,

Macmillan, 1980, and the *Dictionary of Biographical Quota-
tion* (of British and American subjects), published by Routledge
& Kegan Paul, 1978. For quick reference there are the *Penguin
Dictionary of Quotations* and the *Penguin Dictionary of
Modern Quotations*, both compiled by J. J. and M. J. Cohen.
The Concise Oxford Dictionary of Quotations is available in
paperback as a boxed set together with *The Concise Oxford
Dictionary of Proverbs*.

9 The *Writers' & Artists' Yearbook*, published annually by A & C
Black, London. Every writer should possess an up-to-date copy,
and this is one reference book that should be renewed each year.

10 The *Cassell and Publishers Association Directory of Publishing*,
now published annually, and/or *Willing's Press Guide*, published
annually by Thomas Skinner Directories, East Grinstead, W.
Sussex, or *Benn's Media Directory*, 2 volumes, published
annually by Benn Business Information Services Ltd, Tonbridge,
Kent – depending on whether the writer's main interest is in
books or in newspapers and periodicals. The radio and television
writer should have up-to-date copies of the *BBC Handbook* and
IBA's *Television and Radio*. Also recommended are the series
published by Professional Books Ltd of Abingdon, Oxon.: *The
Publishing & Bookselling Directory, The Radio Directory*, and *The
TV Directory*.

11 A dictionary of dates.
Recommended volumes are: *Everyman's Dictionary of Dates*,
7th edition, revised by Audrey Butler, Dent, London, 1985; this
new edition contains a concise chronology of events from 30,000
BC to the present day. Also the *Teach Yourself Encyclopaedia of
Dates and Events*, edited by L. C. Pascoe, English Universities
Press (now Hodder & Stoughton Educational), London, 1974.
The People's Chronology, edited by James Trager, Heinemann,
London, 1979, is a goldmine of information on human events
that are not often found in the more conventional dictionaries.
An older work, which may occasionally be picked up second-
hand for a modest price, is *Haydn's Dictionary of Dates and
Universal Information*, published in 1910, which lists subjects
alphabetically, with information arranged chronologically
under each heading; it contains much of interest that has had to
be omitted from more recent compilations.

12 A concise world history and/or chronology of historical events.
One of the best available in a single volume is William L.
Langer's *An Encyclopaedia of World History*, 5th edition,
Harrap, London, 1973. There is also the useful *Chronology*
series published by Barrie & Jenkins, London, in which events

are calendared each year, month by month, on the left-hand page, while on the right are noted important developments in the fields of politics, science, the arts, sport, etc.; there are separate volumes for *The Ancient World*, *The Medieval World*, *The Expanding World*, and *The Modern World*. Useful for quick reference is S. H. Steinberg's *Historical Tables 58* BC – AD *1978*, 10th edition, Macmillan, London, 1979.

The above titles will form a first-class nucleus reference library, which can be built up over the years according to the dictates of the writer's pocket and his work requirements. Some further suggestions are:

Britain: An Official Handbook, published annually by HMSO, London

Burke's Peerage & Baronetage, 106th ed., Burke's Peerage, London, 1986

Cambridge Historical Encyclopedia of Great Britain and Ireland, The, ed. Christopher Haigh, Cambridge University Press, 1985

Concise Dictionary of National Biography, The, 2 vols, Oxford University Press, 1906, 1982

Concise Guide to Reference Material, ed. A. J. Walford, Library Association, London, 1981

Debrett's Correct Form, rev. ed., compiled by Patrick Montague-Smith, Debrett's Peerage/Country Life/Futura, 1976; paperback, 1979

Debrett's Peerage & Baronetage, new ed., Debrett's Peerage/Macmillan, 1985

Europa Year Book, 2 vols, published annually by Europa Publications, London

Hollis Press & Public Relations Annual, published annually by Hollis Directories, Sunbury-on-Thames, Middx

International Authors' & Writers' Who's Who, 10th edition, International Biographical Centre, Cambridge, 1986

International Who's Who, published annually by Europa Publications, London

Oxford Companion to English Literature, 5th ed., ed. M. Drabble, Oxford University Press, 1985 (Other *Companion* titles are listed on page 88)

Record Repositories in Great Britain, HMSO, London, new ed. due 1987

Shorter New Cambridge Bibliography of English Literature, The, ed. G. Watson, Cambridge University Press, 1981

Statesman's Year Book, The, published annually by Macmillan, London

Whitaker's Almanack, published annually by J. Whitaker, London

Who's Who, published annually by A & C Black, London

Who Was Who, 7 vols published to date, plus a cumulative index volume, covering the years 1897-1970, A & C Black, London

Index

Personal Notes

Personal Notes

Personal Notes

Personal Notes

Personal Notes